PRAYING
with
PURPOSE

Based on the sermons of Fr. Anthony Messeh
Compiled and edited by St. Shenouda Press
with permission from the author

PRAYING
with
PURPOSE

By:

FR ANTHONY MESSEH

ST SHENOUDA PRESS
SYDNEY, AUSTRALIA
2024

PRAYING WITH PURPOSE
By: Fr Anthony Messeh

COPYRIGHT © 2024
St. Shenouda Press

All rights reserved. Except for brief quotations in critical publications or reviews, no part of this book may be reproduced in any manner without prior written permission from the publisher.

All Scripture quotations, unless otherwise indicated, are taken from the New King James Version®. Copyright © 1982 by Thomas Nelson, Inc. Used by permission. All rights reserved.

St Shenouda Press
8419 Putty Rd,
Putty, NSW, 2330
Sydney, Australia

www.stshenoudapress.com

ISBN: 978-1-7635450-6-9

Based on the sermons of Fr. Anthony Messeh. Compiled and edited by St. Shenouda Press. with permission from the author

Table Of Contents

INTRODUCTION 1

PART I: PRAYER ROOMS

CHAPTER 1 - The Simple Prayer 5

CHAPTER 2 - Structured Prayer 11

CHAPTER 3 - Repentant Prayer....................................... 17

CHAPTER 4 - Liturgical Prayer 25

CHAPTER 5 - Thanksgiving Prayer.................................. 35

CHAPTER 6 - Intercessory Prayer 43

PART II: LORD'S PRAYER

CHAPTER 1 - Our Father.. 49

CHAPTER 2 - Hallowed By Your Name 57

CHAPTER 3 - Thy Will Be Done...................................... 65

CHAPTER 4 - Peace In Prayer 73

CHAPTER 5 - Forgive Us Our Trespasses...................... 79

CHAPTER 6 - As We Have Forgiven 85

CHAPTER 7 - Lead Us Not Into Temptation................... 93

CHAPTER 8 - For Thine Is The Kingdom, And The Power, And The Glory... 101

INTRODUCTION

Prayer - Just hearing the word brings a flood of images—hands lifted high, knees bent low, whispered words, or tears streaming down a face. For some, it's an anchor of hope; for others, it's a source of frustration. Let me say something up front: prayer is not just an act we perform. It's not about checking a box or repeating the right phrases. Prayer is a home we build—a sacred place where we meet God, not once in a while but every day.

Now, let me also admit something: prayer is hard. If there's anyone who struggles with it, you're not alone. I'm right there with you. As much as I know that prayer is the answer to everything in life—peace, joy, wisdom, love—I still find myself stumbling. Some days it feels like my prayers bounce off the ceiling. Other days, I get distracted or don't even try. Yet deep down, I know this: every good thing that God wants to pour into our lives, He pours through prayer.

This book is an invitation to something deeper, something real. It's about reshaping how we see prayer—not as a chore but as the place where life with God truly happens. Think of it like building a house. Every house has different rooms, each serving a purpose. There's the family room, for relaxed, heartfelt conversations. There's the living room, where formal, structured prayers take place. The study invites us to connect with God through His Word, and the dining room calls us to pray for others. Finally, there's the bedroom—the place of deepest intimacy, found in liturgical prayer.

Each of these rooms is vital, and together they form the home where we meet God. The process of building that home takes effort, but the reward is this: when you build it, He will come. And when He comes, He brings everything your soul is longing for.

In the second part of this book, we'll sit together and take a fresh look at the Lord's Prayer—the prayer Jesus Himself gave us. This isn't just about analyzing words or memorizing lines. It's about letting the richness of this prayer shape the way we approach God and the way we live our lives.

Part I

Prayer Rooms

Chapter 1

THE SIMPLE PRAYER

Prayer is a means to an end. Think of it as not just an act, but a sanctuary we create. The goal isn't simply to tick the box, "Pray today." The objective is intimacy with God: a communion, a dialogue where we sit together, and He provides all we need. The act of prayer is merely the setting in which this profound connection unfolds. A house serves as a fitting metaphor: owning your own home isn't really the goal, rather the happiness in being with family: sharing meals, having fun, and spending time together. A life anchored in prayer allows God to meet us, fortifying our spirit and being our everything. Building the right spiritual sanctuary is similar to building a real house, each room has a distinct purpose and design. A kitchen is tailored for cooking, while a dining room caters to hosting. In the same way, each aspect of our spiritual life should be crafted with intention.

If we are aware of prayer's benefits, why then do we hesitate? We find time to watch our favorite Netflix shows, exercise at the gym, and send funny tweets and memes. We prioritize these activities, yet often neglect prayer, a practice we genuinely crave. The reason? Our society venerates productivity. We craft lists; completing tasks, making calls, managing chores, and derive immense satisfaction from ticking checkboxes next to each item. In college, I knew someone who epitomized this mindset. During stressful periods, she'd list every task, even sleeping and waking up, eager to check them off. Our culture's obsession with accomplishments has skewed our perception of effectiveness. Consequently, prayer can feel redundant. After moments of reflection, we might perceive no discernible change in our surroundings or within ourselves. This lack of immediate results can deter many especially if we fall into the trap of thinking, "Why pray if nothing seems to change?" Our fixation on tangible outcomes limits our approach to prayer so we must first shift our perspective.

If prayer were transactional – marching into God's house, presenting our demands, and securing immediate responses— we would probably do it more often. However, prayer isn't about issuing mandates, in fact it is the exact opposite in the Bible. It's about approaching God, our Father, in vulnerability, admitting our need for assistance. Consider 1 Peter 5:7: "Cast all your care upon Him, for he cares for you." This verse doesn't promise solutions or checked boxes. Instead it emphasizes the importance of God's unwavering care. As one writer insightfully put it, "Praying means being weak and naive, and that's why we hate it."

What is a good prayer?

What truly characterizes an effective prayer? Is it the length? Eloquence? An authentic prayer isn't measured by its duration or the poetic words used but by its sincerity and vulnerability. As C.S. Lewis aptly put it, "We must lay before Him what is in us, not what ought to be in us." Many hesitate to pray because they believe they lack the right words or sentiments worth presenting to God. Yet, prayer is about unearthing the genuine emotions within us and laying them before God. As Jesus affirmed, "The one who comes to me I will by no means cast out" (John 6:37). Any sentiment, if genuine, is worthy of being presented before God.

Here is the definition of a simple prayer: ordinary individuals presenting ordinary requests to an extraordinary Father. What burdens your heart today? Whatever you feel – be it stress, joy, frustration, or anticipation – God desires to hear it; just as a parent values even the trivial concerns of their child simply because it matters to the child, God values our prayers. Some might argue that prayer should focus solely on worship and service. However, remember, it's better to approach God with the innocence of a child and pray about every little thing than restrict ourselves. As Saint Theresa of Avila insightfully said, "There is no stage of prayer so sublime that it isn't necessary to return often to the beginning."

The Bible is filled with instances of simple prayers as no matter the situation, people always lift their hearts to God:

- **Moses:** He shepherded God's people from slavery to freedom, but at times was overwhelmed by this responsibility. In his frustration he lamented, "Why have you afflicted your servant? Why have I not found favor in your sight, that you have laid the burden of all these people on me?... I cannot bear these people alone; the burden is too heavy. If this is how you intend to treat me, please end my life now" (Numbers 11:11-15).

- **Elijah:** Known for his miracles, he was once was mocked by some youth for his baldness as he walked to Bethel. They yelled, "Go up, you baldhead!" (2 Kings 2:23). In response, Elijah "turned around and looked at them, and pronounced a curse on them in the name of the Lord. And two female bears came out of the woods and mauled forty-two of the youths." (2 Kings 2:24).

- **The Disciples:** "But they did not receive Him, because His face was set for the journey to Jerusalem. And when his disciples James and John saw this, they said, "Lord, do You want us to command fire to come down from heaven and consume them, just as Elijah did?" (Luke 9:53-54). That was their prayer.

These raw and seemingly unrefined prayers by Moses, Elijah, and the Disciples did not stop them from praying spiritual prayers later on. These simple prayers showed that they were sincere, and God accepted them in sincerity and honesty

Practical Tips for Simple Prayer

1. **Strive for the ordinary, not the extraordinary:** Put forward routine, simple prayers and don't try too hard. We often feel that prayer fails when it doesn't move mountains beneath us. Sometimes we do have life-altering prayers, but they don't start that way. We create too much pressure within ourselves to meet this standard. Consider a date with your partner: not every single one will be the most romantic and memorable. Reflect on Psalm 131, "My heart is not proud Lord, my eyes are not haughty. I do not concern myself with great matters or things too wonderful for me. But I have calmed and quieted myself. I am like a weaned child with its mother. Like a weaned child, I am content."

2. **Prioritize consistency over duration:** Our emphasis should be on consistency, not the length of our prayer. Brief, recurrent moments with God throughout the day are more valuable than an hour-long session. Just as we often eat small meals throughout the day or start small and consistently when training for a marathon. This approach also provides regular moments for introspection, helping us recognize and counter our shortcomings. One of St. Anthony's beautiful quotes says, "Calling on the name of Christ, crucified, chase away all the demons you fear as gods." How many of these challenges and temptations weigh us down daily?

3. **Approach God as a father, not a judge:** Prayer is not being summoned to the principal's office or a courtroom. It's like a child eagerly approaching

Santa Claus, expecting only gifts. We go on Jesus' lap, and He's not there to say "Where were you at this time? Why's your Bible dusty?" We are speaking to our Father, and we speak whatever it is that is on our heart, and He listens. The world may label people based on their deeds or status, but God sees everyone as His child. In Matthew 6:6, it's written, "Pray to your Father who is in the secret place; and your Father who sees in secret will reward you openly." A parent's love remains constant, whether a child is soaring high or facing challenges. We should never confront life's problems alone but invite God to be part of the solution.

4. **Understand Jesus is always accessible:** Regardless of our state of mind or the situations we face, Jesus is always within reach. While on this earth, He associated with all: from tax collectors to Samaritans, even attending a wedding at Cana and visiting Lazarus's tomb. There's no place or situation He would shy away from. Since His birth in a humble stable, Jesus has shown He will go anywhere and be with anyone, especially the downtrodden, traitors or the rejected. In moments of isolation or struggle, remember Hebrews 4:15: "For we do not have a High Priest who cannot sympathize with our weaknesses, but was in all points tempted as we are, yet without sin."

Simple prayer embodies the essence of ordinary individuals making ordinary requests to an extraordinary Father. Every situation, no matter how mundane or challenging, invites Jesus to accompany us. While some may see simple prayer as elementary, it is foundational for a balanced prayer life. A home wouldn't be built without a family room, where one can relax and be their true self. Similarly, our relationship with God needs us to be sincere, honest, vulnerable and weak, and that's the beauty of simple prayer.

Chapter 2

STRUCTURED PRAYER

Prayer is a topic many of us acknowledge needing to engage in more frequently. This is no surprise, yet many of us struggle to consistently cultivate a strong prayer life. This is the core conflict which doesn't make sense: even though we understand that prayer can be a major contributor to our success, we often neglect it. We're aware of the power of prayer, how it can achieve and assist in various situations, and how it serves as our connection to God. Therefore, our goal must be to "reframe" our perspective of prayer: instead of seeing it as just another act or task, we should make it a building project, constructing a 'house of prayer' within ourselves. When this house is built correctly, it becomes our meeting place with God, where we earnestly believe He will consistently reveal Himself because of the foundation we've set.

If we don't view prayer as merely a task, we can truly grasp its essence and see it as a relationship: dedicated time spent with God. It's important to realize that while prayers might change due to the external situations we're worried about, our ultimate goal is internal transformation. Our focus must shift from external priorities to personal growth.

The house of prayer we build is the place we go at set times during the day, to act in set ways and is a part and habit of our everyday life – what we have called the simple prayer. As we mature, we slowly expand our prayer house, now introducing a structured prayer. While this may feel foreign compared to the usual simple prayers, expanding our 'house of prayer' is essential for our spiritual journey.

When we first return to our relationship with God, the initial reunion is marked by miraculous and wonderful feelings. We become acutely aware of God's presence, especially after a prolonged absence from Him. In the beginning, our prayers are often self-centered, reflective of our infancy to prayer. As newcomers to the world of prayer, we lack an understanding of structured prayer. Still, God recognizes our earnest attempts, welcoming us with open arms, encouraging our endeavors, and rewarding our sincerity. Yet a time comes when the simplicity of our initial prayers must evolve: we begin to add layers to our spiritual foundation, not discarding what we've learned but enhancing it. This progression signifies our ability to express gratitude when God blesses us and maintain faith when He doesn't. This is the stage where our prayer habits mature, transforming from spontaneous appeals to structured prayers – sessions we commit to even when we aren't necessarily in the mood.

God aims to teach us that prayer isn't merely a channel to obtain our wishes. It's a deeper bond, a dynamic relationship where God provides, withdraws, instructs, and reveals Himself to us. As described in Romans 8:29 by St. Paul, God's ultimate aspiration for us is to embody the likeness of His Son. Jesus Christ is presented as our model: our mission is to mirror Christ's choices, deeds, and entire essence. Thus, to comprehend our destined appearance and nature, we turn to Christ. God's eternal plan for us remains the same: we who were perfect are broken through sin and what God wants is for us to be perfect again in His Image. St Gregory of Nazianzus says "Let us become like Christ, since Christ became like us. Let us become gods for His sake, since He for ours became man." In His grace, He chose to resemble us and embrace our humanity, making it possible for us to partake in His divinity. He sacrificed His riches so that we, in our poverty, might be enriched – such is God's purpose for us.

Attaining Christ-likeness isn't an overnight transformation. Nor is it a daily task to be crossed off a list, but a profound and continuous spiritual journey. Some moments of conversion – like the epiphany of the Samaritan woman upon encountering Christ – are instantaneous, but true spiritual maturity unfolds over a lifetime. Just as child-birth is a distinct period separate from a child's growth and maturity. Our spiritual journey starting is immensely valuable to God, but it must continue to grow. All of us desire unwavering faith in God, peace amid chaos, and love in the presence of animosity. But these virtues demand a lifetime of cultivation. Hastily developed 'quick fix' spirituality will disappear just as swiftly. However, if we nurture our spirit consistently it becomes robust and resilient in the face of challenges. Once again – it doesn't happen overnight! Genuine growth and transformation mandates regular practice, rooted in daily habit changes. Such dedication, repeated until it becomes our norm, leads us closer to becoming Christ-like. "You also, as living stones, are being built up as a spiritual house, a holy priesthood, to offer up spiritual sacrifices acceptable to God through Jesus Christ." (1 Peter 2:5) Saint Peter emphasizes that if we want to construct a spiritual house, a sanctuary of prayer, it needs to be built one stone at a time. He likens these spiritual stones with the Old Testament's priesthood and sacrificial system which followed specific guidelines – they were conducted at designated times, in a set manner, accompanied by specific prayers. This system is the blueprint for maintaining a structured prayer life.

So what is Structured Prayer?

As we now know, simple prayer forms the foundation by which we communicate with God: whenever we feel compelled, using our own words. This spontaneous prayer is essential. Still, there's a need to also pray during times when we're not particularly inspired, when prayer doesn't come easily. Hence, the importance of structured prayer at specific times and specific words. God introduced the idea of structured prayer with designated times and words in the Old Testament: "Now this is what you shall offer on the altar: two lambs of the first year, day by day continually. One lamb you shall offer in the morning, and the other lamb you shall offer at twilight. ... This shall be a continual burnt offering throughout your generations at the door of the tabernacle of meeting before the Lord, where I will meet you to speak with you."(Exodus 29:38-43).

The idea of structure may seem restrictive, conjuring images of rigid rituals, but it doesn't have to be negative. We all have daily rituals, be it eating, working, studying, or dressing. These routines help us achieve specific goals. Some might argue that rituals render prayer meaningless, however expressing sentiments like "I love you" daily to a loved one is in itself a ritual, but it's far from meaningless. Rituals merely provide a framework. The sincerity and meaning within that framework are up to us. The Pharisees, whom Christ admonished, weren't criticized for their rituals but for their hollow repetitions. He instructed them on the right approach, emphasizing the importance of genuine and structured prayer.

Structured prayer addresses common challenges in spiritual life, like inconsistency and imbalance. Just as parents guide their children on proper habits such as brushing teeth or eating, structured prayer guides us. It's a consistent practice, whether or not we're inspired in the moment. As Metropolitan Anthony Bloom teaches, "Spontaneous prayer (simple prayer) is possible in two situations; either at a moment when we have become vividly aware of God… or when we become suddenly aware of the dire peril we face approaching God."

Structured Prayer

Believing that we can rely solely on spontaneous prayer for our entire lives is naive. Genuine spontaneous prayer emanates from deep within, either from awe or distress. It doesn't arise from those in-between times when we aren't particularly moved by divine presence or consumed by the gravity of our situation. Attempting spontaneous prayer during such times is never works. Another common hurdle in prayer is uncertainty about what to say. We find ourselves distracted, neither in awe nor distress. While spontaneous prayer is valuable, there are times we struggle with words. That's where structured prayer provides a framework, offering words to articulate our connection with God, especially when we feel lost or restless.

Even if set words aren't inherently ours, when they reflect our inner feelings, we can reliably embrace and infuse them with our sincerity. So, why not draw from the Psalms of King David, whom God deemed "a man after My Own Heart"? David's profound connection with Christ assures us that his words can enrich our prayers. When praying with structure, we don't mechanically recite; instead, we contemplate the profound meanings behind the words. This deeper engagement elevates our prayer life. When we're familiar with the words and not preoccupied with recalling them, our minds are free to focus on their true essence.

The Agpeya is a blessing to us. It spans the day, beginning with the first hour at 6am and extending until midnight. Each hourly prayer incorporates Psalms from the Old Testament, Gospel passages from the New Testament, and an assortment of written prayers and litanies. This book provides structured words and prescribes specific times for us to connect with God. Challenge yourself: allocate 12 minutes to God daily. Practice praying three times—morning, midday, and evening. For each session, use words from a different hour and dedicate four minutes to the act. In the first hour prayer of the Agpeya, we pray Psalm 69: "Hasten, O God, to save me; O Lord, come swiftly to help me... I am poor and needy; come quickly to me,

O God." These words perfectly capture the times in our lives where we cannot pray, where we cannot stand before God; when we don't know what to say or what to think. The words of King David express our own feelings and we say save us quickly, we are poor and needy.

Consistency in these structured prayers is crucial as steady prayer serves as a vehicle for long-lasting transformation. Developing the required discipline of prayer nurtures it into a habit which lets us emulate the discipline of Christ. "But we all, with unveiled face, beholding as in a mirror the glory of the Lord, are being transformed into the same image from glory to glory, just as by the spirit of the Lord." (2 Corinthians 3:18). When Moses received the Ten Commandments, he spent 40 days atop a mountain. During this time, he neither ate nor drank and remained in the divine presence. Upon returning to his people, he was profoundly changed and his face was radiant, reflecting his deep transformation.

Our ultimate purpose therefore is to mirror Jesus in our lives. While spontaneous prayers have their place, structured prayers instil a deeper discipline within us, driving us closer to our objective of reflecting God's image. Through prayers, we seek transformation in every aspect of our life: turning our hate to love, pride to humility, and anxiety to trust. Once again, this will not happen overnight, but with a firm commitment to routine time with God, we will achieve inner transformation which we are promised by God. The true goal is that internal change that ensues when we pray.

Chapter 3

REPENTANT PRAYER

As we established, prayer isn't merely an act, but rather a house we live in to communicate with God "To be conformed to the image of His Son." Each room in this house is designed for a specific purpose; the simple prayer room for a candid outpouring of our worries and feelings to God, and the structured prayer room for a deliberate allocation of time for spiritual communion. The next room in this house is the repentant prayer room.

Rewiring our minds to align with Christ's thoughts is a gradual process. Transforming our anxieties into trust, or our gaze into one resembling Christ's – full of purity and compassion – takes time. Imagine taking long, direct airplane flight. Peering out the window, the scenery view of sky and clouds doesn't really change so it's impossible to tell how much progress you've made. That's precisely why inflight maps exist – to reassure passengers about the journey's trajectory, as a small change in angles would lead to big problems! Similarly, in our spiritual journey to be more Christ-like, even a minor deviation can lead to significant challenges over time. Thus, continuous spiritual recalibration is crucial. King Solomon's words in the Songs of Solomon 2:15, "Catch us the foxes, the little foxes that spoil the vines," highlight that often it's the small distractions, not the major ones, that veer us off course. For instance, Judas didn't start off as a traitor: he was one of the chosen twelve, present during many of Christ's miracles. However, small deviations in his life like greed and pride led him astray. The Greek term for sin, "Amarteya," which literally translates to "missing the mark." What is the mark? The mark is Christ. Contrary to popular belief, sin isn't just doing bad things – it's any deviation from the path set by Christ.

The Greek term "Pemthos" in the Bible doesn't have a suitable English equivalent. While it can be described as "mourning" or "sorrow," it signifies a Godly mourning, "a broken and contrite heart" (Psalm 51:17). When Jesus said, "Blessed are those who mourn, for they shall be comforted," He referred to this divine sorrow. Such godly mourning brings divine comfort and blessings. St. Anthony the Great stated, "Whoever wishes to advance in building up virtue will do so through weeping and tears." This doesn't suggest constant misery which is sometimes how it is interpreted. After all, Jesus was the most joy-felt and upbeat person in the world. We know this because children loved to hang out with Jesus, and children don't like to hang out with miserable people. Thus, mourning doesn't oppose joy. Acts 2:37 also uses the word "Pemthos": "Now when they (people of Israel) heard this, they were cut to the heart, and said to Peter and the rest of the apostles, 'Men and brethren, what shall we do?'" This is the essence of a broken spirit, being repentant and asking what to do out of the brokenness of our hearts.

The phrase "broken and contrite heart" signifies an awareness that our inherent sinfulness distances us from the complete presence of God. Imagine God inviting you into a special room of prayer, yet you're unable to step inside due to your state of sin. True repentance goes beyond the sins we commit; it addresses the state we're in. We are not sinners because we do sinful things, we do sinful things because we are sinners. Whether on days you err frequently or not at all, the need for repentance remains. This isn't about sinful deeds but about the deep-seated realization of our sinfulness. When we compare our flawed nature with God's immaculate essence, our shortcomings — pride, ego, selfishness, injustice — become glaringly apparent. This broken and contrite heart is the realization that I cannot stand next to God, and due to this sinful nature inside me, I cannot stand in the same picture as God, I ruin the picture!

This recognition evokes a profound sense of self-awareness and humility. St. Paul, in Romans 7:15-20, details how his inherent nature occasionally steered him towards wrongdoing, even when he largely led a righteous life. Like St. Paul, we all grapple with this intrinsic sway towards sin, like a car veering off course when we let go of the steering wheel. Straying momentarily away from the path of righteousness is human, but the longer the deviation, the harder it is to return. Taking the wrong exit on the motorway is not a big problem if you notice straight away, but if you notice two hours later it will take much longer to get back. Once we embrace the Spirit we received at baptism, we are given additional strength to combat this tendency. The goal then becomes empowering our divine Spirit to overcome our old nature. Our old nature might recede, but sadly will never entirely disappear, lulling us into complacency and ready to resurface later. St. Paul finishes off the passage by saying "O wretched man that I am! Who will deliver me from this body of death?" (Romans 7:24). The answer is that God will deliver us through repentance.

Living a Life of Repentant Prayer

"Pursue peace with all people, and holiness, without which no one will see the Lord" (Hebrews 12:14). The call isn't to achieve perfection but to strive for purity. Matthew 5:8 reinforces this by stating, "Blessed are the pure in heart for they shall see God". Many passages in the Bible teach the relationship between repentance and prayer. In the Old Testament, before entering the Holy of Holies, a sanctum where God would meet his people, there was the bronze laver. Here, priests washed their hands while viewing their reflection in mirrors, using self-reflection as a means to preparation for purification. Similarly, during Holy Liturgy, priests wash their hands whilst praying the Psalm of repentance. In John 13 during the last supper Jesus "laid aside His garments, took a towel and girded himself... and began washing the disciples' feet". Why would he stop the meal for washing? Because the rule is: in order to enter the Holy of Holies, you must wash first. Peter's reluctance to have his feet washed by Jesus is met with "if I don't wash you, you have no part with Me".

The overall level of repentance in our prayers is weak, and I'm the first to admit it. It's not just about saying sorry for our wrongdoings. True repentance is a spirit and life of repentance, a life of a broken and contrite heart, recognizing our unworthiness in front of a Holy and almighty God. We should approach God in prayer with the sentiment, "God, have mercy on me, a sinner." By humbling ourselves in God's presence, He lifts us and cleanses us. The good news is that even if we lack this deep spirit of repentance, we can develop it. How do we foster this attitude in our prayers? Our church fathers emphasize that humbling oneself before God is our strongest defence against the devil. The devil can't follow us when we humble ourselves. Scripture frequently mentions the grace God bestows upon the humble. Just like the bronze laver and the washing of the feet, before we enter into the Holy of Holies we must (figuratively) wash in the following ways:

- **Seek Guidance:** How can we nurture a repentant spirit? Ask God for it. Simple prayer is foundational. As St James mentions, we often lack because we don't ask. Start with a genuine plea: "Lord I'm not good at repentance, give me a broken and contrite heart" even if you do not know what it means.
- **Self-reflection:** It's easy to notice others' flaws while overlooking our own. I, for instance, am meticulous when hunting for online deals, even for

something trivial like socks – I read the fine print, delivery charges, returns policy, everything! Yet, I neglect to examine my own soul with the same microscope. Our priorities are skewed when we're more concerned about saving money than the state of our souls. Anything in our life without examination or evaluation will come to ruin. "The Lord searches all hearts and understands all the intent of the thoughts" (1 Chronicles 28:9). The reason our spiritual lives are weak is because we are unaware of our true state, and we spend so much time analysing and focusing on the wrong areas leaving us zero time evaluating our own souls.

Our spiritual life should be fenced by a gate with two functions – to keep the bad things out, and let the good things in. Sins of commission are the bad things that we do such as, "I yelled at this person", "I lied to this person", "and I cheated this person". Sins of omission are the good things that we fail to do such as failing to minister to someone when an opportunity arises.

- **Confession:** True confession involves admitting our sins to God and those we've wronged. Some confess in the church but forget to talk to God, while others do the opposite. We must do both. The tax collector in Luke 18:13-14 make excuses, attempt to justify his sins, or blame others for his sins. But rather he stood before God and had the Pemthos, the broken heart and said, "God forgive me, I'm a sinner". And the Bible proceeded to tell us that this man went to his house justified that day.

- **Engage with God:** Repentance prepares us for being near to God with God, just like with prodigal son's repentance led back to his Father's embrace. If Jesus had only washed the feet of His disciples and sent them off, it wouldn't have been the same. He washed their feet and invited them to participate in the partaking of His Body and Blood. Our prayers should draw us closer to God, not keep us at a distance.

- **Act in Obedience:** Repentance requires action. If you've wronged someone, rectify it. True repentance demands more than words; it requires action. Share your struggles and seek forgiveness, as suggested in James 5:16: "Confess your trespasses to one another, and pray for one another, that you may be healed". One of the reasons why we don't understand God's forgiveness is because we don't share our struggles with others. We don't give people the chance to administer forgiveness for us and be the vehicle for our forgiveness.

The Purpose of Repentant Prayer

Repentant prayer isn't about wallowing in guilt or leading a life of misery. Instead, it's akin to the feeling of washing away dirt and sweat during a shower. This refreshing sensation is precisely what repentant prayer offers. Without experiencing this spiritual cleanse, we remain burdened and distant from the joy God intends for us.

Have you heard about Shrek the sheep? Shrek was a sheep in New Zealand discovered in a cave after having been lost for years. Though a typical sheep's fleece weighs around 10-15 pounds, Shrek's weighed a staggering 60 pounds. After being sheared, he looked as good as new. Shrek symbolizes what happens to us when we neglect our spiritual cleanliness.

There's no reason God's children should be burdened with spiritual dirt. If we had a God who didn't forgive, or if grace wasn't accessible, or if spiritual cleansing was unattainable or costly, perhaps one could justify not seeking purification. However, with a God who earnestly invites us to be cleansed, saying, "I will wash you, make you pure, and remove your burdens, distancing them as the east is from the west," there's no reason to refuse His offer.

Hosea 6:1-2 articulates the spirit we must embrace: "Let us return to the Lord; for He has torn, but He will heal us; He has stricken, but He will bind us up. After two days He will revive us; on the third day He will raise us up; that we may live in His sight." This spirit is crucial, particularly if it's been a while since we last sought spiritual cleansing.

The next time you pray, add a spirit of repentance, the spirit of a broken and contrite heart. Take 30-60 seconds of silence, and remind yourself that you are a sinner, and that He is a holy God, and make a prostration, then begin your prayer. Enter into the presence of the Lord in a new spirit.

Chapter 4

LITURGICAL PRAYER

On a long family road trip in a cramped minivan, by the time you arrive at the destination everyone is exhausted, eager to use the bathroom and eat something. My goal is always to get everyone settled in their rooms as quickly as possible, turn off the lights, and finally reach my own bedroom, thinking, "Ah, I've made it." Similarly, in our house of prayer, the equivalent final room we use at the end of the day is our place of rest, our place of intimacy with God.

When my daughter was in second grade, she transitioned to a new school as we had just moved home. There was an event – one of those school functions parents are almost obligated to attend. Since my wife was working, I, with my flexible schedule, decided to go. It was my first time attending such an event. Eyes were already on me when I arrived late, after the show had already started, plus my 'unusual' black priest garment made sure that I drew immediate attention. To add to the awkwardness, my daughter was in a phase where she didn't want photos taken of her. She had an unspoken rule: "You can attend, but don't take pictures, or even glance my way." So here I am, I walked in late, dressed like the 'weird' guy, standing in the corner not even allowed to look at my daughter. I'm just waiting for security to come and apprehend me. A lady came toward me and said: "Excuse me, can I ask you a question?". When someone frames their query this way, I know which three words are coming next: "What are you?" if I am in one of my moods I can play around with this, I can mess with the person. But in this situation, I said let me play it safe and just said "I am a priest." "What's a priest?" she asked. And then we started to chat. Her genuine curiosity about my faith led to a discussion about our Sunday worship practices, the liturgy, the Holy Communion and other rituals. As we conversed, she became more passionate, comparing our practices to those of her church. Then she remarked something poignant, a million-dollar phrase that I wrote down and will always remember, questioning the authenticity of her church's practices: "Is this really how they worshipped in the New Testament?" The result of that conversation was three things: we invited her to our house for dinner, she invited me to speak at her women's Bible study group, and (very importantly) security was not called that day.

The Need for Liturgical Prayer

Reflecting on this spiritually dedicated lady: she'd done mission trips, served in her church and adopted multiple children who came from different situations, yet surprisingly she was frustrated with her church. Yet, I understand and even anticipate such feelings. Here's why: I firmly believe that our souls yearn for liturgical worship, which is the final room in our house of prayer we crawl into at the end of our day. Just as I can't find true rest on a road trip until I reach my bedroom, our souls remain restless until they engage in liturgical prayer. Our very existence isn't about us; it's about our Creator. We were fashioned with a divine purpose in mind – to worship and unite with God and only in this unity can we function optimally. Regular liturgical worship helps us realize this, reminding us of Revelation 3:20: "Behold I stand at the door and knock. If anyone hears My voice and opens the door, I will come in to him and dine with him, and he with Me." Intimacy and oneness dining together, this is what we were made to do.

Before delving deeper, let's clarify: what exactly is 'liturgy'? While now commonly associated with religious ceremonies, such as the Eucharist or Mass, the term 'liturgy' itself doesn't mean anything spiritual but rather a group of people working together for the same purpose. It embodies the spirit of teamwork. Thus, feeding the homeless or cleaning a park can both be termed a 'liturgy'. In the context of the Orthodox Church, it denotes collective prayer or sacraments. For instance, Sunday services are termed 'liturgy of the Eucharist', indicating the sharing of bread and wine as body and blood. Baptisms, funerals, and various sacraments all fall under this category of liturgy.

For our purpose, think of 'liturgy' as a room, and the act performed within the liturgy as an event. Using the bedroom analogy, while the bedroom is the physical space, the intimacy shared through communion is the event. It's essential to distinguish between the place (liturgy) and the activity (communion) because our goal is not the liturgy, our goal is the communion. The very concept of the Eucharist traces back to Scripture, specifically Matthew 26. It is Jesus who instituted the liturgy of the Eucharist. He "took bread, blessed and broke it, and gave it to the disciples, saying, "Take, eat; this is My body." He then took the cup, gave thanks, and shared it, saying, "Drink from it, all of you. For this is My blood of the new covenant, which is shed for many for the remission of sins." We replicate this act weekly.

If you're unfamiliar with Orthodoxy or are exploring it, you may wonder, "Is he being metaphorical?" as you read the following, but please bear with me as I explain. I'm not speaking in metaphors. We believe that every Sunday, we gather to partake in the very real body and blood of Christ. It's not just symbolic; it's a mystery. And by 'mystery', I mean understanding the 'what' without grasping the 'how'. Take a murder mystery, for instance: we know the butler was killed, but how? That's the mystery. Similarly, in the Eucharist, the bread is Christ's body. The details? It's a mystery. Perhaps I mean this symbolically? No, John 6:53 reinforces the literal interpretation: "Most assuredly, I say to you, unless you eat the flesh of the Son of Man and drink His blood, you have no life in you. Whoever eats My flesh and drinks My blood has eternal life, and I will raise him up at the last day." Later, it is emphasized, "For My flesh is food indeed, and My blood is drink indeed." (John 6:55). Believe me this message is not metaphorical.

For those raised in the church, if someone says "we eat His body and drink His blood" they respond with something like "bring it on. We love that." But non-church people are more likely to respond with "I beg your pardon?! I've walked into one of those kind of churches... That's kind of weird." If that's you, you're not alone in feeling this way. When Jesus introduced this concept two millennia ago, many found it strange. As we read in John 6:60, some disciples remarked, "This is a hard saying; who can understand it?" Yet, my plea is that you don't hastily retreat like those who didn't understand, "From that time many of His disciples went back and walked with Him no more." (John 6:66), who abandoned Jesus due to this challenging teaching. Ask yourself: if Jesus meant this metaphorically, would he have let them go due to a misunderstanding of an analogy?

The key to understanding the Eucharist is not to fixate on the mechanics. This is not a science experiment which we are going to dissect. It's a matter of faith, trusting in Jesus's words that His body and blood are genuinely present. The Eucharist is the fulfilment of Christ's ministry on earth. Every action of Christ led to the Eucharist, and our actions lead us to it as well. But why? To comprehend Christ's mission on earth, consider this: was His primary goal to baptise, to provide Scriptures, or merely to sacrifice Himself? Of course these were vital steps, but St. Paul illuminates the deeper intent in Colossians 1:26-27: "The mystery which has been hidden from ages and from generations, but now has been revealed to His saints. To them God willed to make known what are the riches of the glory of this mystery among the Gentiles: which is Christ in you, the hope of glory." The ultimate aim was to reunite God and humanity, re-establishing the unity they once enjoyed in Eden. What Moses couldn't figure out, what David never saw, and what Solomon only dreamed about seeing, was revealed through Christ's arrival and the ensuing events, culminating in the Eucharist, to achieve this unity. God will live in man again, through the Holy Spirit, and that's exactly what happens every time we gather for the Eucharist. We re-live Christ's death, His resurrection, His ascension, and we ask the Holy Spirit to descend upon us and upon this bread.

The great orator, preacher, and father of the church, St John Chrysostom says this, "We receive within us the same body of our Lord Christ that was born in the manger of Bethlehem, the same body that walked on the sea of Galilee, the same body that was crucified on Calvary, the same body that was resurrected from the tomb, the same body that ascended into heaven and now sits on the right hand of the Father. There is no power in life greater than this." From the outset, early Christians recognized the Eucharist as Christ's ministry's culmination. It embodies His death, resurrection, ascension, and the arrival of the Holy Spirit. For us, the Eucharist signifies the profound unity between God and us.

The question you may now be asking is, "Ok I'm all about the bread and the wine, and all about Christ in us. But why does that require liturgical prayer." We have been describing the event, and now let's consider the room. Why the structure? Why the incense? Why stand for long durations? Why every week instead of once a month? Is it merely symbolic or truly His body? Why is communion typically set in the context of liturgical prayer?" Questioning is good... but the key when asking these questions, is to make sure you ask the right person. It's natural to ask one another or even oneself, but we should be asking God directly. Instead of deciding how we want to connect with God, shouldn't we ask how He wishes to connect with us? After all, worship is directed towards Him, not for our personal satisfaction. Imagine you have to buy a birthday present for someone. You'd ask, "Whose birthday is it? Is it your Dad's birthday or your son's birthday?" The answer dictates your choice. Similarly, in worship, shouldn't our focus be on what God desires rather than what we prefer? The reality today is that the majority of churches out there are worshipping God the way they want, not the way God wants. That's why some will have this worship style and then after some time they'll change and say they want a new worship style. Why is it changing if the recipient is an unchanging God? And as the people change, and the audience changes, the worship continues to change, and many people – like the woman I mentioned earlier – struggle with that. But in Orthodoxy, we do not have that problem because we don't change. Some may challenge this and say, well who says God wants it that way. Doesn't God just care about spirit? Doesn't God just want us to be sincere? Does it have to look a certain way? Can you ever find a place where God is clear and says this is how I need to be worshipped? Absolutely! The entire Old Testament.

In the book of Exodus, we see the first time that God gave instructions on how worship should be performed. "Take one young bull and two rams without blemish, and unleavened bread, unleavened cakes mixed with oil, and unleavened wafers anointed with oil (you shall make them of wheat flour). You shall put them in one basket and bring them in the basket, with the bull and the two rams…" (Exodus 29:1-3)."You shall also take one ram, and Aron and his sons shall put their hands on the head of the ram; and you shall kill the ram, and you shall take its blood and sprinkle it all around the altar. Then you shall cut the ram in pieces, wash its entrails and its legs, and put them with its pieces and with its head." (Exodus 29:15-15). He continues until he says at the end, "Thus you shall do to Aaron and his sons according to all that I have commanded you." (Exodus 29:35). Reading these passages, it's clear that there's very little room for deviation: God has been explicit about exactly how He wants to be worshipped. Why? Because

Liturgical Prayer

He wants to be worshipped in a way that befits His glory, not a way that pleases us. We are not the audience, we are the giver and the giver doesn't determine the gift, the recipient does. Thus liturgical worship remains the same because the recipient remains the same: the unchangeable, everlasting, infinite God.

Let us explore another two reasons that highlight the need for the liturgical aspect of worship.

- **Biblical Worship:** It's essential to note that liturgical worship is, indeed, biblical. And by "biblical", I'm not only referring to the Old Testament, which is undeniably clear on the matter. But what about the New Testament? Do we see hints of liturgical worship there? The answer is a resounding yes. Consider the breaking of bread: this consistent theme was evident several times – on the road to Emmaus, during Jesus' time with His disciples, after His resurrection by the sea, and with Saint Paul on the ship to Rome. The early church rightly believed this was truly His Body and Blood, and it wasn't till 6 centuries later that the misinformation of 'symbolic' Body and Blood began.

    Another explicit description of liturgical worship in the New Testament can be found in Acts 13:2: "As they ministered to the Lord and fasted, the Holy Spirit said, 'Now separate to me Barnabas and Saul for the work to which I have called them." The term 'ministered' used here in Greek is 'Leetorgonton', which is the same as 'Liturgy'. It signifies more than just everyday ministry; it points to communal worship or corporate prayer. And the fasting that precedes it is distinctive to how we perform our liturgy of the Eucharist. This was in about 50AD, two decades after Christ's death and resurrection on earth, and we see signs of the early liturgy in the Scripture. For those who find liturgy boring, I have one famous response:

you're boring. Liturgy is Spirit-filled, it is dynamic. Liturgy is where the Holy Spirit is speaking, its lively, its fire, it's alive. Just because you haven't experienced it (yet), doesn't mean it doesn't exist.

- **Heavenly Worship:** This underscores the grandeur of liturgical worship. By "heavenly" I mean it literally represents what worship looks like, sounds like and feels like in Heaven. While I haven't personally seen heaven first-hand, we have accounts from those who paint a vivid picture. Hebrews 8 and 9 hint at this: "...there are priests who offer gifts according to the law; who serve the copy and shadow of the heavenly things..." The Old Testament provides a shadow, a vague silhouette of heavenly worship. But the New Testament brings it into clearer focus, revealing more about the true nature of worship. Consider the events in Christ's life, such as his betrayal by Judas. These occurred first, and then prophets in the Old Testament foretold them. This tells us that heaven is the ultimate reality, and our present actions mirror what exists in heaven. We're not determining the future; heaven already exists in its perfect form. The Old Testament provided a foreshadowing, and our current era, represented by the New Testament, mirrors that reality.

Two individuals shared their visions of the kingdom of Heaven. The first was John in the Book of Revelation, and the second was the prophet Isaiah. John describes his vision in Revelation, "Around the throne were twenty-four thrones, and seated on the thrones were elders dressed in white robes with golden crowns on their heads" (Revelation 4). This is similar to the image of a priest in a white Tonya we see every Sunday service. He continues, "And from the throne proceeded lightning, thundering, and voices. Seven lamps of fire were burning before the throne, which are the seven Spirits of God. Before the throne there was a sea of glass, like crystal. And in the midst of the throne, and around the throne, were four living creatures full of eyes in front and in back." (Revelation 4). He speaks of these creatures, reminiscent of a lion and a bull, akin to our deacons, who continually exclaim, "Holy, holy, holy is the Lord God Almighty, who was, and is, and is to come! (Revelation 4:4-8)." This again echoes our Sunday liturgy.

Isaiah shares his divine vision in chapter 6. He recounts, "I saw the Lord sitting on a throne, high and lifted up, and the train of His robe filled the temple. Above it stood Seraphim; each one had six wings: with two he covered his face, with two he covered his feet, and with two he flew. And one cried to another and said: "Holy, holy, holy is the Lord of hosts; the whole earth is full of His glory!" This very chant is recited in our churches every Sunday. Isaiah further says, "And the posts of the door were shaken by the voice of him who cried out, and the house was filled with smoke." This smoke resembles the incense used in church. Some might dismiss incense as mere tradition, but it's deeply symbolic. Baby Jesus got three presents for Christmas and one of them was incense. You take away incense and you take away one-third of His Christmas gifts. Incense isn't about our preferences but how God wishes to be honored. Isaiah continues, "Then one of the Seraphim flew to me, having in his hand a live coal which he had taken with the tongs from the altar. And he touched my mouth with it and said: 'Behold this has touched your lips; your iniquity is taken away, and your sin is purged." (Isaiah 6:1-7). Or said in another way, "given for the remission of sins and eternal life for those who partake of it." This is what we do every Sunday – this heavenly experience mirrors our Sunday ritual.

An ordained priest, symbolising an angel, approaches and offers the sacraments for the forgiveness of sins, granting eternal life to those who partake. We have fellowship together, we sing songs, we preach. That's all great. But the pinnacle of what we come to liturgy for is this healing touch.

The gift we offer to God every Sunday is not the bread and wine, it's ourselves in the bread and wine. The bread and wine are just the tangibles. In that bread, I put my repentance, I put my gratitude, I put my request, I put my faith, I put my entire life; my cares, my anxieties, my worries, my fears, my future, my past. Liturgical prayer is where we exchange our lives for the life of Jesus. We come and say, "God, everything we have, we come and put it here on the altar." And he says, "Everything I got I put it back in there." We are invited to pour ourselves into that bread, all the earthly things we have, and He pours everything He has from Himself. As Elder Sophrony, a 19th-century sage, aptly noted, "In the liturgy, we present our transient lives with all their intricacies. In return, God grants us His eternal life. Our emotions, gratitude, repentance, intercessions - our very soul - are imbued in the offerings of bread and wine. And God, in His grace, infuses His divine essence into these gifts and returns them to us."

Chapter 5

THANKSGIVING PRAYER

In our house of Prayer that we are building, our goal is to get to the final room (our bedroom) which represents our intimacy with God our creator; firstly however all other rooms must be tended to first. As we go through our house, we realize that our prayer life becomes increasingly harder and more difficult. Challenges to our will: how we make time for God, how we want to be in the image of Christ (structured prayer), how we want to be clean (repentant prayer), how want to have guidance and wisdom (prayer through Scripture). Thanksgiving prayer is a challenge of faith, not will.

Giving thanks can prove to be a bitter medicine, especially when our inner voice protests, "I don't feel like it now." Yet, I am convinced this resistance is precisely what many need to overcome. In today's world, many are drowning in negative emotions like anger, bitterness, and self-pity. When such individuals are encouraged to praise God, their retort often begins with, "Why? Let me tell you what God did to me." It is in these moments we must intensify our prayer, transforming our challenges into opportunities for healing through praise and gratitude. We must remind ourselves what prayer is about: prayer is the human response to the love that

God pours upon every soul. We love because He first loved us. Prayer isn't a means to earn His love; rather, it's a way to reciprocate it. Therefore, if prayer is a response to God's love, then the purest form this can take is through thanksgiving and praise.

The Bible uses phrases such as give thanks to the Lord, praise the Lord, bless the Lord, magnify the Lord, and honor the Lord. All these words mean different things, however, they fit into the same genre of asking for nothing, and seeking only to honor and glorify God. Thanksgiving is the essence of all prayer but should also be distinctly reserved as a selfless act of worship.

When my family and I take our post-Easter vacation, it is a time of relaxation, comfort, joy and rest. One year we were staying in a beach house and on the first morning, I felt very compelled by God to wake up early, and spend some quiet time on the beach. I began to read 2 Corinthians 12, which is a passage about the grace of God. All of a sudden, it all clicked: I felt like I finally understood the grace of God. The verse said "My grace is sufficient for you, for My strength is made perfect in weakness". I then had an urge to get up and start walking: at 5am I walked a mile and a half, praying to Him and singing praises. I spent two hours on the beach that morning, and I didn't ask God for anything. I felt like for the first time in my life, I understood what the grace of God was, and then I naturally overflowed with thanksgiving and praises.

Take a moment to recall a time when you were similarly moved to praise and thank God. Teaching gratitude, like instructing my children to say "thank you," is about recognizing His kindness, not about emotional display. The Bible directs us to "praise the Lord" and "give thanks to the Lord" (Psalm 106). The truth of the matter is that we serve a great God, our God cannot be contained in the heavens and the earth, our God is immeasurable, infinite and His attributes are unfathomable. If we are not praising Him and appreciating who He is, we should re-examine our spiritual lives. Our goal is to achieve a balanced house of prayer. We cannot have praise but no repentance, or repentance without Scripture. Herein lies a crucial aspect that merits our attention to improve.

In many homes, the dining room is that seldom-used space reserved for special occasions. Similarly, our approach to thanksgiving prayer may be infrequent and reserved for when we want to offer thanks or ask for something specific. Often, our prayers are repetitive: "Thank you, God, for all you've done; you're the best. Now, give me..." We tend to bypass this 'dining room' because we feel that the occasional acknowledgment in our prayers is sufficient, leading us to feel out of place or awkward when we do decide to use it. However, the practice of praise should be a frequent and consistent part of our lives. Recognizing the good that God has done, acknowledging our blessings daily, and understanding our fortune to have Him as our Father are critical to a healthy spiritual life. Forgetting the greatness of our Father and His generosity, or failing to regularly offer thanks and praise, indicates a self-centered, ignorant, or indifferent attitude.

The Bible places great emphasis on praise and thanksgiving. For example, "Enter His gates with thanksgiving, and His courts with praise." (Psalm 100:4). It's about seeking nothing but appreciation for who He is and His deeds. In the Old Testament, King David even assigned a group in the tabernacle solely for the purpose of giving thanks and praising God (1 Chronicles 16:4). King David commands us many times throughout the Psalms to praise and give thanks. This highlights just how important gratitude is in our spiritual duties. Looking even further back when God gave the system for sacrifices, He said that one of the sacrifices is called a "thank offering" (Leviticus 7:12), again highlighting the importance of gratitude. One should ask why praise and thanksgiving are so emphasized? Does it imply that God is a dictator, or demands adulation due to arrogance or insecurity? Just as a parent who teaches their child to say "thank you" for a sandwich, it's about instilling appreciation and recognition that has its benefits:

Praying With Purpose

1. **Expression of our faith:** First and foremost, praise and thanksgiving are expressions of faith. If we don't regularly engage in these practices, our theological understanding is flawed. Theology is tested not just in reciting the Nicene creeds or snippets of Scripture like "All things work together for good to those who love God" (Romans 8:28), but by maintaining praise and gratitude through tough times. If you believe that "all things work together for good to those who love God", then put yourself in that category and thank God even if things aren't working. It's in the moments when we face challenges that our true belief is revealed. Take Job, for example. Despite facing immense adversity, he remained steadfast in his faith, as seen when he responded to his wife's despairing remarks with conviction, refusing to blame God (Job 2:9-10). Similarly, the apostles Paul and Silas, despite being beaten and imprisoned, prayed and sang hymns to God (Acts 16). Their faith was not shaken by their circumstances; it was demonstrated through their actions and led to a miraculous release and conversion of the jailor and his family. True belief in God manifests through praise and thanksgiving, regardless of circumstances. It's not merely professed; it's lived.

2. **Finding Joy in Sorrow:** It's been psychologically proven that the words we speak can shape our thoughts. This suggests that by choosing our words carefully, we can transform our mindset. During times of distress, when gratitude seems farthest from our minds, compelling ourselves to give thanks and praise can pivot our attitude and perspective, leading us to discover joy amidst sorrow. Consider the perception of barrenness in Old Testament times – it was seen as a curse from God. People equated God's love with the number of one's children, believing more offspring signified greater divine affection. Isaiah 54 addresses a barren woman who is shunned and despised, with

an empty home and a resentful husband, a woman with seemingly no hope for change. What advice does this passage offer to this woman who is probably miserable? God's counsel is unconventional: "Sing, O barren, you who have not borne! Break forth into singing, and cry aloud, you who have not labored with child! For more are the children of the desolate than children of the married woman" (Isaiah 54:1). Here, God challenges the woman's beliefs, implying that faith and praise in adversity will bring blessings surpassing those in better circumstances. In God's way, it isn't, "I give you and then you praise", it is more like "you praise, and I will give you".

Similar was the experience of Moses, with God's promised land, peace, and rest contingent after crossing the Red Sea, not before. Our struggle often mirrors this; we seek comfort and tranquility before making our own leap of faith, yet true rest awaits on the other side. The lesson is clear: cease our complaints, abandon bitterness, and trust in God – that is when we find our own promised joy. "Stop telling God how big your problems are and start telling your problems how big your God is." Instead of dwelling on the size of our challenges, we should confront them with praise and gratitude. With each new obstacle, our response should be one of worship and thanksgiving.

3. **Delighting the Heart of Our Father:** "If we could only see the heart of God, if we could only see the heart of the Father, then thanksgiving and praise would never leave our lips." God is not a lifeless entity or a robot who is up there just to answer prayers. As we are created in His image, we share His capacity for emotion. When God embodied flesh in Jesus Christ, He embraced our human feelings. When His children express gratitude, as shown in Luke 17, it brings Him joy. After healing ten lepers, only one, a

Samaritan, returned to offer thanks. Jesus expressed a poignant longing for the absent gratitude of the nine, highlighting that no act of thankfulness, no matter how small, escapes God's notice. God cherishes our acts of thanks, no matter how small. They are a reflection of our understanding of His boundless love. Let us not reduce God to a stoic figure; He is above all else, a loving Father.

Practical Steps to Begin

Allow me to share three tips to get you started. Remember, the only way to do a prayer wrong is to do it insincerely. If the prayer is insincere, it will be wrong no matter what you do, and if it is sincere, the prayer will be right no matter what you do.

1. **Start small:** Don't begin with grandiose declarations of God's omnipotence or omniscience – concepts that may feel distant or abstract – but rather with the tangible aspects of life for which you're genuinely grateful. Set yourself a task for the week: write down five different things you're thankful for each day. This practice, starting with modest appreciations, paves the way for a spontaneous heart of gratitude for all God's works.

2. **Use Psalms from the Agpeya:** This book of structured prayer is priceless. Use the ninth hour because it is full of Psalms of praise. "Sing to the Lord a new song..." (Psalm 96), "Make a joyful shout to the Lord..." (Psalm 100), all of them are songs of praise. God said that David's heart was the closest to His heart, so when we learn from David by using His Psalms, we aim to get to that same place.

3. **Sing songs:** There is something powerful about music and song, touching our emotions and soul in ways mere words cannot. Often, people recount feeling God's presence most profoundly during musical

worship. As it is said, "music is the language of the soul." Like a persistent tune, music can captivate us. Ephesians 5:19 encapsulates this: "Speaking to one another in Psalms and hymns and spiritual songs, singing and making melody in your heart to the Lord, giving thanks always for all things to God the Father in the name of our Lord Jesus Christ."

Regardless of your starting point – be it with simple gratitude, the Psalms, or song – it is crucial to begin. As stated in 1 Thessalonians 5:16-18: "Rejoice always, pray without ceasing, in everything give thanks; for this is the will of God in Christ Jesus for you." For those seeking God's will, it is plainly expressed here: rejoice, pray, and give thanks. Let us channel our energy, often spent battling problems, into the uplifting act of praise. Draw closer to God, magnify Him, and I assure you, the return on this investment of worship will surpass any solitary struggle with life's challenges.

CHAPTER 6

INTERCESSORY PRAYER

Intercessory prayer focuses on the well-being of others rather than ourselves, and appreciating the importance of praying for those around us. The benefits of such prayers are not strictly for us, but they can greatly aid others (which is why it's a challenging practice). It involves people we know and care about; we bring them into our prayers and advocate on their behalf. Some might question why we should pray for others when we rarely pray for ourselves! Yet this form of prayer is a step toward true intimacy with God. Our love for others naturally leads to intercessory prayer. Many of us often wish to give more than we can to those we care about. This desire brings us to a crucial realization: prayer can magnify our ability to help our family, friends, and those who are poor, sick, or oppressed. Although our own actions have limits, prayer invites God's boundless power into their lives. We must consider what God is willing to do for them and recognize that our prayers can significantly impact people's lives.

The essence of intercessory prayer is that it extends our capacity to make a difference beyond what we could imagine. While we can offer advice, share sermons, and provide spiritual resources, it is through our intercessory prayers that we can truly influence our neighbors' lives. Many around us suffer from anxiety, abuse, doubt, and a lack of faith, but our prayers can be a catalyst for change. If we see a transformation in someone's life as a result of our prayers, we should not feel guilty for not having prayed sooner; rather, we should commit to not delaying our prayers or support for others in need. We must use the power of prayer entrusted to us by God, as neglecting it holds us accountable.

As we read in James chapter 5, Elijah was an ordinary man, yet his earnest prayers stopped the rain for three and a half years. Then, he prayed for rain, and the heavens responded. "The effective, fervent prayer of a righteous man avails much." (James 5:16). Intercessory prayer isn't for the faint-hearted or those seeking personal gain, but for those who are willing to strive for meaningful change in the lives of those around them. Intercessory prayer needs the attitude of a servant of God.

The Need for Intercessory Prayer

In both the Old and New Testaments, God outlines the duty of the strong to aid the weak. The strong are to support the poor and the able are to assist the less fortunate. In the Old Testament, access to God was limited, as Christ was yet to bridge the gap. Thus, designated intercessors like Aaron stood in prayer before the Lord for the people's sake. "So Aaron shall bear the names of the sons of Israel on the breastplate of judgment over his heart, when he goes into the holy place, as a memorial before the Lord continually. So Aaron shall bear the judgment of the children of Israel over his heart before the Lord continually." (Exodus 28:29-30). Similarly, Samuel's commitment to pray for the people was not just out of the goodness of his heart, but rather that omitting this was a sin against God: "Moreover, as for me, far be it from me that I should sin against the Lord in ceasing to pray for you; but I will teach you the good and the right way." (1 Samuel 12:23).

Intercessory Prayer

In the New Testament, the duty to intercede extends to all believers, not just the priests. "You also, as living stones, are being built up a spiritual house, a holy priesthood, to offer up spiritual sacrifices acceptable to God through Jesus Christ." (1 Peter 2:5). Jesus' arrival tore down the barriers between us and God, granting us the role of intercessor just like Aaron and Samuel. Our church is tasked with spreading the gospel, praying for all, and accounting for every individual as Jesus does for us. Our duty now is not only to pray for those who cannot pray for themselves but to ensure no one is forgotten, resembling Jesus' ministry. Jesus takes these prayers and fulfills them: "This is My commandment, that you love one another as I have loved you." (John 15:12).

Jesus' role in the universe, between us and God, is to be the mediator, the intercessor and to ultimately bring us back to God. St. Ambrose reminds us that without Jesus' intercession, we cannot know God intimately. When we pray in Jesus' name, we do so because it is as if He Himself is petitioning on our behalf. It is for this reason we pray and say "In the Name of Jesus Christ". It is fitting therefore that we follow Christ's example, we must intercede for others, bringing them closer to God. It is through shared compassion and unity in prayer that we prepare ourselves for a deeper intimacy with God. Our love for others reflects our love for God, and indifference toward their suffering indicates a disconnect with the heart of God.

Understanding our duty to intercede is one thing; knowing how to effectively carry it out is another. True intercession goes beyond mere requests for God's presence and blessings for our neighbors; it requires the right attitude, a system, and the support of Christ.

1. **Attitude of persistence:** Moses exemplified an outstanding attitude of persistence in intercession. He stood before God on behalf of Israel – whether they sinned, were in need, or faced adversaries – and God responded. "And Moses said to Joshua, "Choose us

some men and go out, fight with Amalek. Tomorrow I will stand on the top of the hill with the rod of God in my hand." So Joshua did as Moses said to him, and fought with Amalek. And Moses, Aaron, and Hur went up to the top of the hill. And so it was, when Moses held up his hand, that Israel prevailed; and when he let down his hand, Amalek prevailed. But Moses' hands became heavy; so they took a stone and put it under him, and he sat on it. And Aaron and Hur supported his hands." (Exodus 17:9-12). Moses prayed while Joshua fought, but it was Moses who became exhausted from his intercession!

It's often easier to offer practical help than to maintain a fervent prayer life. We like immediate results, but prayer works differently. It's a process that requires perseverance, especially when the outcomes are not immediately visible. Luke chapter 18 teaches this through the parable of the persistent widow. "Then He spoke a parable to them, that men always ought to pray and not lose heart." (Luke 18:1). The message is clear: faith in prayer should be unwavering. Just as the widow persevered, we're called to do the same, to labor in prayer with faith, even in the absence of immediate results. Prayer is not a light switch, but ploughing the ground, working tirelessly day in, day out, with the same effort as before.

2. **System of intercessory prayer:** without a system our intercessory prayers can be inconsistent: great results one day then nothing on another. One such system is a "Prayer Card". This is a focused prayer tool that includes the names of individuals or groups, accompanied by relevant Bible verses and specific prayer requests, allowing for updates, reminding us of the situation we are praying for.

A prayer card example for the group Suffering & Hurting: "He heals the broken-hearted And binds up their wounds. He counts the number of the stars He calls them all by name." (Psalm 147:3-4). Then list names of those struggling physically, psychologically or maritally.

Other category examples include Family, Church Leadership, Work, World's problems and so on. Keep a concise amount of cards and pray a set group each day. Take each group and go through them thoughtfully and prayerfully. The more thought that has gone into the card, the more you will be able to say in prayer and the better the intercession will be. When we pray for someone we feel more connected to them, and we can speak stronger to our neighbor because we have shown we love them in our intercessory prayer. Add a card anytime and expand it progressively and use this system to assist in your intercessory prayer.

3. **Support of Christ:** When we intercede, we join Christ in His work. We do not simply pray for others; but more vividly we become Christ's hands, speaking on His behalf. Christ advocates for us before the Father, seeking healing and restoration. Remember, in intercession, you are an extension of Christ's mission.

Intercessory prayer transcends duty. It's not solely about the people we pray for, but about serving God and joining Him in His work on Earth. Our task is to work alongside Jesus, who tirelessly intercedes, until our final day. Christ is the head; we are the body. As part of Christ's body, we are each responsible for its well-being. Just as an ailment in one hand affects the whole body, so do the struggles within the Body of Christ affect us all. We are called to be fellow laborers with Christ, carrying the burdens of the Body in prayer.

Part II:

Lord's Prayer

Chapter 1

OUR FATHER

Everyone, regardless of age, shape, or background, seeks peace in life. Curious about the lengths people might go to find peace, I typed "peace" into Google to see the top ten results. The search yielded various results, from self-help software to music. One particularly interesting result was a photo marketed as a "picture of stillness." Other notable mentions included aroma therapy, a "peace of mind" plumbing service, and uniquely named services like '20-minute miracle seaweed, melt away the mental block of life.' It's evident that people are inventing myriad ways to attain peace. Considering the rising stress levels in society, with many stating that today's populace is more stressed than any previous generation—especially in areas like the DC metropolitan area—it's no wonder the search for peace is paramount.

So, where does one truly find peace? The Bible, a timeless source of wisdom, offers guidance. Philippians 4:6-7 says, "Be anxious for nothing, but in everything by prayer and supplication, with thanksgiving, let your requests be known to God; and the peace of God, which surpasses all understanding, will guard your hearts and minds through Christ Jesus." Simply put, the Bible suggests that the key to inner peace is prayer. Through prayer, we discover the unparalleled peace of God.

How should one pray? While the initial answer might seem straightforward—prayer leads to peace—it's essential to delve deeper. Yes, the Bible advocates that through prayer, we can achieve it, but is it that simple? Most of us have prayed, yet not all experience that peace. So, it's not just about praying; it's about understanding how to pray effectively. Prayer requires practice and dedication to refine. How, then, should we approach prayer? What words should we use? What posture is appropriate? Where should our focus lie? Does attire matter? These questions guide us in seeking the true essence of prayer. These are common and important questions. Have you ever genuinely pondered these, or have you simply mirrored the practices of others—repeating their words, kneeling when they kneel, or expressing emotions as they do?

The good news is that we're not the first to grapple with this question. Once, when Jesus walked the Earth, His disciples posed the same query, saying, "teach us how to pray." Jesus answered by presenting the Lord's Prayer. But this wasn't just a set of words to be repeated endlessly. It served as a model, illustrating the essence of prayer. A prayer we utter in every service. Using 'Our Father' as a guideline, we notice it comprises several distinct prayers. When combined, they reveal a divine blueprint for prayer—a kind of prayer leading to peace. Let's begin with its opening phrase, as mentioned in Matthew 6:9: "In this manner, therefore, pray: Our Father in heaven." This seemingly simple phrase encapsulates a revolutionary concept and is foundational to achieving a peaceful life. By instructing us to address the supreme Creator, the Master of galaxies and the universe, as 'Our Father', Jesus was introducing a radical shift.

You might wonder, "What's so revolutionary about calling God 'Our Father'?" The significance lies in its rarity in older Scriptures. Throughout the extensive history chronicled in the Old Testament—spanning thousands of years—God is referred to as 'Father' merely seven times. While other titles like 'Lord' or 'Creator' are frequent, 'Our Father' is exceptionally scarce. But this paradigm was precisely what Jesus aimed to transform. In the Gospels alone, this endearing term appears over 150 times. Just within Matthew 6, it's used seven times.

So, when Jesus said to address God as "Our Father"—akin to saying 'Abba', 'daddy', or 'papa', a deeply affectionate term—he was breaking long-held beliefs. This shift from viewing God as a distant, omnipotent figure in the heavens to recognizing Him as an intimate, caring 'Father' was groundbreaking. Jesus wanted to convey that God isn't merely a distant force or a disinterested creator. He emphasized the loving, nurturing nature of God as our Father. This revelation is profoundly comforting. A force remains distant and unrelatable, however, with a Father, there's an opportunity for a deep, meaningful relationship—a connection that's genuine and nurturing.

The challenge with understanding God as our Father is that each person's perception of "father" is influenced by their own relationship with their dad. For some, this evokes feelings of warmth and nurturing, while for others, it might bring up memories of absence, anger, negligence, or dishonesty. As children, many of us experienced moments of dread associated with our fathers. For instance, in my childhood, while my mother was the more lenient parent, my father was the stricter one. If we misbehaved, my mother would warn us with the phrase, "Wait till your father comes home." As the evening approached, our behavior would invariably improve, anticipating our father's return. This association can sometimes create a barrier when we talk about God as our Father. If someone's predominant emotion toward their dad is fear or disappointment, they might resist the idea of God being a father figure, thinking, "I've had enough of one father; I don't need another."

It's not uncommon for children to perceive God as perpetually displeased, always demanding more. For example, if they pray, they might feel God expects them to pray even more. Such feelings could stem from their relationship with their earthly fathers. In the U.S., statistics indicate that 24 million children grow up in homes without a father. Consider the impact on their perception when they hear the phrase "God is your Father." Interestingly, a study I came across highlighted 50 renowned atheists, including figures like Karl Marx and Freud. A surprising commonality among them was their strained relationship with their fathers. This raises an intriguing question: If someone lacks a positive fatherly bond, does it hinder their ability to connect with God, fundamentally seen as our Father? We must work towards separating our experiences with our earthly fathers from our understanding of God as our Father. Grasping this concept is vital. If we don't recognize and embrace the unique, loving relationship God offers, we might never truly experience the solace that prayer can bring.

What kind of Father is God? Let's look at His four characteristics:

A caring God

God's care for us is boundless, surpassing our comprehension. The vastness of His love is something our minds can't grasp fully. To attempt explaining God's love is akin to teaching calculus to a baby. Just as a baby cannot fathom the intricacies of calculus, we, as humans, struggle to grasp the depth of God's affection. Psalm 103:13 says, "As a father has compassion on his children, so the Lord has compassion on those who fear Him." If asked to define God in one word, many would say love, compassion, or care. These sentiments shine through in all depictions of Him.

Recall the Gospel story where the disciples were in a boat with Christ. When a storm arose, and the boat rocked, Christ slept peacefully. In their panic, the disciples woke Him, questioning, "Don't you care that we're in danger?" Can we truly say we understand God's nature if we haven't pondered whether He cares about our everyday concerns? From our studies to our social lives, from our joys to our sorrows, does God truly care? 1 Peter 5:7 provides an answer, "Cast all your anxieties on Him because He cares for you." This isn't about selectively handing over a few worries but entrusting Him with all our burdens, be it significant or mundane. The word "cast" here doesn't mean to throw lightly, like with a fishing line, but to offload a weighty burden, trusting that God can bear it. Reflect on Matthew 6:31-32, which advises against worry, stating, "Do not worry, saying, 'What shall we eat?' or 'What shall we drink?' or 'What shall we wear?'" It continues, "For your heavenly Father knows that you need all these things."

A crucial realization is that only one can carry the weight of our worries – either it's us or God. If you're analytical, like me, you might wonder why God insists on carrying our burdens. Wouldn't it be easier for Him if we managed our issues? Yet, God is not a distant figure; He's our Father. Imagine a child, anxious about basic necessities like food and clothing. Such worries would break a parent's heart, making them feel they've failed. Similarly, when we stress about our needs instead of trusting God, we inadvertently suggest that He's not capable of caring for us. Our actions should reflect our belief in a God who cares, ensuring we don't portray ourselves as spiritual orphans. As children of God, it's important we recognize our worth and live as heirs to His kingdom. The central message? Our God is not just powerful or distant; He is a caring Father.

A consistent Father

The second key characteristic of God is His consistency. This means we can always rely on Him. As stated in James 1:17, "Every good gift and every perfect gift is from above, and comes down from the Father of lights, with whom there is no variation or shadow of turning." In contrast, earthly fathers can be unpredictable. One day they might say, "Yes son, let's go to the game!" and the next, they're too busy. Their moods can fluctuate based on events like their team winning or the stock market's performance. This inconsistency in earthly fathers stands in stark contrast to our Heavenly Father, who remains steadfast every day.

If you observe insecurity in people today, particularly among the younger generation, it often stems from the lack of consistency they experienced with their fathers. This lack of stability can lead to feelings of insecurity, both in earthly relationships and in our spiritual connection with God. Many misunderstand God's nature. They fear that a sin committed yesterday might invite punishment today. This is a misconception. God isn't waiting for a chance to punish. Had He intended to, considering our countless transgressions, He would have done so already. But He remains consistent, even when we falter.

While human relationships can be transactional – where kindness is often reciprocated and mistreatment is met with coldness – God's love remains unwavering. No matter how many times we stray from His teachings, His love and care for us remain unchanged. This sentiment is echoed in Malachi 3:6, where amidst the world's inconsistencies, the Lord declares, "For I am the Lord, I do not change; Therefore you are not consumed, O sons of Jacob." It's evident: God's nature is unchanging. Recognizing this consistency is crucial when we approach Him in prayer. Misunderstandings or unmet expectations often lead to resentment, both towards fellow humans and God. For instance, children can deeply resent parents who break their promises, leading to significant household strife.

Similarly, some harbor misunderstandings about what God promises. Resentment builds when they feel He hasn't delivered on presumed promises like happiness, popularity, or success. However, we must understand that God hasn't defaulted on any promises. What He assures, He delivers, like the promise in Philippians 4 which states that consistent prayer will bring God's peace into our lives.

A close father

In Acts 17:27, we see that God is always within our reach: "they should seek the Lord, in the hope that they might grope for Him and find Him, though He is not far from each one of us." Contrary to the notion some might have, based on experiences with absent earthly fathers, God is never distant. He is never too preoccupied or unavailable. This perception is reinforced by a study Time magazine conducted, comparing parental time spent with children between 1970 and 2005. The study revealed that parents today spend an average of 22 hours or less per week with their children, a noticeable decline from previous decades. Sometimes, societal pressures might prioritize work, leisure, or other commitments over spending time with family. But God is different. Imagine if our prayers were met with a 'busy' tone — thankfully, it's not so with Him. Whether He is metaphorically reading a newspaper or watching TV, God is always ready to engage with us. He is never 'busy'; He is always near, always attentive. This closeness is crucial for effective prayer, as emphasized in Psalm 145:18: "The Lord is near to all who call upon Him, To all who call upon Him in truth." Recognizing God's availability strengthens our faith in prayer. Approaching Him without this conviction can hinder our spiritual connection.

Consider the relationship between a father and his child: a loving parent will repeatedly tend to a child's needs, no matter how recurring. Similarly, God is ever-present for us, be it for guidance, solace, companionship, discipline, or any other need. He never tires of assisting, no matter the frequency. Drawing from personal experience, I've always been ready to care for my child, even though I'm an imperfect parent. Matthew 7:11 encapsulates this sentiment perfectly: "If you then, being evil, know how to give good gifts to your children, how much more will your Father who is in heaven give good things to those who ask Him!"

While I, as an earthly father, might have my shortcomings yet am willing to do everything for my child, think of how much more our flawless Heavenly Father is willing to offer. Always remember: God is close. Never believe He'll dismiss your concerns or turn you away. He remains ever-present.

A competent God

God is not just caring, consistent, and close, but what truly stands out is His competency as a Father. While He deeply cares, He also possesses the power to act on that care. Many individuals in life might care for you and stay close, but their capacity to help is limited. In contrast, there isn't a problem God cannot address. We might sometimes feel our mistakes are beyond redemption, but rest assured, no situation is beyond His capability to mend.

Turning to pop culture, the portrayal of fathers on television often lacks depth. These TV role models shape a perception that, while fathers (and by extension, God) might have good intentions, their capacity to help might be limited. This couldn't be further from the truth. Recall Luke 1:37: "For with God nothing will be impossible." This belief is vital when approaching Him in prayer. Recognize His unwavering presence and limitless capability.

Consider your most significant challenge now, regardless of its nature. Reflect on Ephesians 3:20: "Now to Him who is able to do exceedingly abundantly above all that we ask or think, according to the power that works in us." God's power surpasses our wildest imaginations. Even what seems insurmountable to us, God can address effortlessly. Jesus highlighted this intimate relationship when He taught us to approach God as "Our Father," emphasizing closeness rather than superiority.

Chapter 2

HALLOWED BY YOUR NAME

As in the prayer from Matthew 6:9, "Our Father in heaven, Hallowed be Your name," our focus shifts to the phrase "Hallowed be Your name." Two questions come to mind when reflecting on this phrase. Firstly, what does "Hallowed" mean? Growing up, I mistakenly thought it said, "Halloween thy name." After understanding the term "Hallowed," the second inquiry arises: Why is it vital to hallow the name of someone, and more specifically, why hallow God's name?

The term "hallow" can be described as setting something apart as holy, sanctifying it, or regarding it with immense respect and reverence. With this understanding, we must ask: Why is it crucial to hallow God's name specifically, as stated in "Hallowed be Your name," instead of just "Hallowed be God"? How does this relate to finding inner peace?

It's evident that many people frequently utter God's name without reverence. Often, they use His name casually in daily conversations, sometimes even as an exclamation of frustration or as a curse. Consider how it might feel to be referred to thoughtlessly, devoid of respect. For God, whose name embodies holiness, such usage can't be pleasing.

This emphasizes the importance of truly understanding and upholding the sanctity of His name. In the biblical era, names held profound significance. They weren't merely labels chosen by parents; they revealed an individual's identity, role, or lineage. For instance, a person named Joe Carpenter likely had ancestors who were carpenters. Similarly, a "Michael Jackson" would have been recognized as the son of someone named Jackson. Names weren't just designations; they depicted who you were. This same importance applies to God. Each name attributed to Him in the Bible reflects a different facet of His character. When Christ speaks of hallowing God's name, He isn't just referring to a title. He means honoring and revering God's very essence. Recognizing and respecting God, beyond just His name, acknowledges His overarching character.

The act of hallowing God's name offers more than just reverence. It aids in reducing life's stresses. Beginning our prayers by connecting with God and subsequently recognizing His greatness and essence not only fosters a deeper spiritual bond but can also alleviate our worldly burdens. Let us explore how recognizing and respecting God's name can diminish our stress:

1. When we honor God's name, we acknowledge His power to fulfill our deepest needs. In the Old Testament, there are numerous names used to describe God, indicating more than just the identity of "God." With each revelation of a new facet of His character, He would introduce a new name. For instance, "Jehovah Shalom" translates to "God is my peace." So, when God perceived the people's longing for peace, He revealed Himself as "Jehovah Shalom," underscoring His role as the ultimate giver of peace. Another designation God introduced is "Jehovah Sincanu," or 'God is my righteousness.' Jeremiah 23:6 reflects on this, proclaiming, "Now this is His name by which He will be called: THE LORD OUR RIGHTEOUSNESS." In the original Hebrew text,

the phrase would be "Jehovah Sincanu." These names symbolize different aspects of His nature. They affirm that God is the resolver of issues and the absolver of guilt. Beyond these examples, the Bible contains numerous other names for God, such as the helper, provider, and the Almighty. Each of these names addresses a unique human need.

Often, stress stems from seeking inappropriate solutions to problems. For example, relying on something incapable of bearing the burden we place on it. Many times, we mistakenly expect other people to satisfy needs only God can fulfill. This flawed reliance is evident even in marital expectations. I often advise couples that their partner, regardless of their deep love and commitment, cannot fulfill every need; only God can. Relying excessively on people for our needs only sets the stage for heartbreak. I recall a feature on ESPN Classic about John McEnroe, the renowned tennis player. Interestingly, the spotlight wasn't on his tennis prowess but his ex-wife, Taylor O'Neil. She spoke of her unfulfilled yearning for love from her parents and how she now seeks it in her children. Such expectations are recipes for disaster. When we look to others to satisfy needs only God can address, we are courting disappointment.

The critical question is: if you've identified a need, who are you relying on to fulfill it? The most immediate and pressing need is often one only God can meet. If we don't recognize this and shift our burdens onto Him, we risk a life riddled with anxiety, devoid of true peace. Prayer is our gateway to this realization. Beginning a prayer by acknowledging God as our Father and honoring His name sets the foundation. A question that often arises is, if God knows our needs, why doesn't He automatically provide? The truth is, prayer isn't about informing

God of our needs. He's already aware. Instead, prayer is about demonstrating our trust and reliance on Him. It's a testament to our faith. Thus, when we venerate God's name, we're reminded of His capacity to cater to our deepest desires.

2. When we hallow God's name, we recognize that God is greater than our challenges. Consider the most daunting hurdle or seemingly insurmountable issue. Both you and I understand that any problem, no matter its size, has a solution. Entering a prayer with significant challenges means you will leave prayer recognizing the enormity of God. With the reverence of God's name, you present your issues, but leave with an understanding that God far surpasses them. Your immediate problems may persist — the stock market might still be down, your pockets may remain empty, relationships could be strained — but in the grand scheme, God overshadows even your gravest concerns. This is the peace derived from centring on God's name. Focusing on it offers a renewed perspective on life.

Often, our prayers resemble a laundry list of requests. While God hears every plea, such a list may not grant you the desired peace. Jesus taught us to "Hallow thy name" for a reason: it diverts our attention from immediate problems to the omnipotent force behind them. Obsessing over issues magnifies them; but by revering God's name, you appreciate His vastness, and your concerns become trivial in comparison. Just a few moments reflecting on God's might diminishes the weight of our problems. He sculpted the oceans, rivers, and existed since time immemorial. And here we are, stressing over temporary troubles. Connecting deeply with God, rather than rattling off requests, nurtures our relationship with Him. Imagine, for instance, you call your spouse, listing chores without any personal interaction. "Do the laundry, do the dishes, pick up the dry cleaning, take out the trash, put the kid to sleep, I'll be home at 10." Would that be a good way to further the relationship between partners? No way! Such an approach hardly fosters a loving relationship, nor does it with our relationship with God. King David understood this saying, "Let them praise the name of the Lord, For His name alone is exalted; His glory is above the earth and heaven" (Psalm 148:13). He realized the name signifies the person. Respecting and honoring God's name places everything into perspective, reminding us that our issues are not the universe's focal point. Similarly, in Psalm 31:3-4, another common description for God emerges: "For You are my rock and my fortress; Therefore, for Your name's sake, Lead me and guide me." God is often likened to a steadfast rock. People across the world travel to marvel at grand rock formations. Why? Their enduring, unyielding nature commands respect. For inner peace, let God be your rock. Regardless of life's turbulence, God remains an unshakable foundation. Everything else may be unstable, but with God as your rock, nothing can shake you.

Consider your current pressing problem, be it guilt, insecurity, anxiety, a bad habit, or any challenge. All that goes on top of the Rock and the Rock can solve it. When you comprehend God's greatness and resilience, you recognize that no issue is insurmountable. 1 John 3:20 reinforces this: "For if our heart condemns us, God is greater than our heart, and knows all things." On days when doubt consumes us, this truth is a solace. Even when our own heart seems like the enemy, God is our unwavering ally. By hallowing God's name, we realize His infinite power to solve anything.

Consider the story of Job. Job's narrative is among the earliest in the Bible, and it's certainly a long and depressing one. The tale revolves around Job, an upright man who experiences an unparalleled string of misfortunes. Tragically, he loses his family, wealth, children, livestock, and even his home. Throughout the story, Job continuously questions God, asking, "Why?" His friends, too, weigh in, often offering misguided counsel. What's peculiar about this book is God's response. After a prolonged silence and as Job suffers immensely, God finally confronts him. But rather than answering Job's "Why?", God recounts the history of His creations. He reminds Job of His omnipotence, saying, "I crafted the Earth, sustain the universe, and have governed the world long before you existed and will continue to do so eternally." God emphasizes His grandeur, control over natural wonders, and other magnificent feats.

Despite not receiving the answer he sought, Job finds solace. Not because God assured him of problem-solving, but because God showcased His supremacy over every challenge. Job realized that God's might surpassed even the gravest of problems. If you're sceptical, I encourage you to read the concluding two chapters of Job. There, you'll see that Job departed with a newfound peace, grounded in recognizing God's vastness. So, whenever you feel dwarfed by life's challenges, remember: God's greatness eclipses all.

When we hallow God's name and treat it as sacred, we acknowledge that He invites me into His family. The profundity behind "Hallowed be Your name" is truly enlightening. This magnificent name of God, so revered and holy, is what He bestows upon us once we become part of His kin. The very same name, held in such awe, becomes part of our identity. He labels us Christians, calls us His sons, daughters, and children. Just as parents pass on their surnames to their children, God grants us His name as a testament to our bond. This association means we embody His reputation; we become His ambassadors. While our characters remain inherently unique, our actions shape God's reputation. This distinction is crucial. Ephesians 2:19 encapsulates this sentiment, proclaiming that we are "members of the household of God." If the son of a king acts dishonorably, it tarnishes the family's name. Similarly, if a child's attire causes others to judge their family's financial status, it affects the family's image. Many people, having been wronged by those who carry the name of Christianity, distance themselves from it. A striking example is Gandhi, who famously remarked, "I would become a Christian if it weren't for the Christians."

Being endowed with God's name is a monumental honor. Missteps in our conduct may lead others to misconstrue God's nature: our actions either honor or tarnish His name. The overarching theme is clear: we must live a life that brings honor to God's name, whether we're on a basketball court, at the airport, or stuck in traffic. Indeed, there's a significant weight to carrying God's name, reminiscent of the saying, "With great power comes great responsibility." Yet, the responsibility shouldn't be burdensome. If it feels so, there's a crucial element missing: love. Upholding God's commandments devoid of love is a daunting task. Doing so might even lead to resentment. But remember, Christianity is about mutual love between us and Christ. When love is the driving force, adhering to His teachings becomes a joy, not an obligation. In essence, hallowing God's name is an act of reverent love.

Chapter 3

THY WILL BE DONE

Next we delve into Matthew 6:10, "Thy will be done On earth as it is in heaven." Our focus is how praying for God's kingdom can usher in peace. Indeed, achieving lasting peace is no easy feat. It's fleeting; you could feel it throughout the day or over a weekend, but a single midnight call, an unexpected trip, or a brief interaction with someone can disrupt it. Having peace one moment doesn't guarantee its presence the next.

There are three situations where we often lose our inner peace:

1. **Uncontrollable Circumstances:** Events like illnesses, traffic jams, or tragedies like September 11th can rob us of our peace simply because they're beyond our control.

2. **Unchangeable People:** Ever tried to change someone resistant to change? Such endeavors can exhaust you, turning your hair grey or driving you to the edge in no time.

3. **Unexplainable Problems:** Frustration builds when things don't operate as they should, and we can't understand why.

However, embracing the prayer, "Thy kingdom come. Thy will be done On earth as it is in heaven," can be a pathway to rediscovering that peace. Of all the lines in the Lord's Prayer, this one often perplexes many. People frequently ponder its meaning. What does "Thy kingdom come" entail? How do we define God's kingdom? Why do we desire its arrival? Where does it currently reside, and how will it transition here? How does this phrase relate to God's will manifesting on earth as it does in heaven?

To put it simply, when viewed with an earthly lens, a kingdom refers to the domain over which a king or queen holds authority. It's marked by defined borders where everyone adheres to the ruler's laws. Similarly, God's kingdom is any realm where He reigns supreme. It's where God commands and is recognized as the Lord.

Contrary to popular belief, God's kingdom isn't on this earth. Instead, our world is filled with chaotic forces, resulting in ailments like cancer and other miseries. Though God's presence can be felt through believers, our world is distinct from heaven. In heaven, nothing defies God's will. However, a prophesied day will come when Christ returns to claim the earth as His kingdom, where every being will acknowledge His majesty. Until that day, God's kingdom on earth is manifested through us. When we crown God as the ruler of our hearts and homes, His dominion is established. Similarly in a church, many believers unite under God's banner, forming a collective kingdom. It's essential to recognize that while evil persists, this earth isn't entirely God's kingdom.

The statement "Thy Kingdom come" is explained by "Thy will be done": where God's will is actively carried out, His kingdom is established. Whenever individuals adhere to God's will, His sovereignty is affirmed. As highlighted in Philippians 4, to experience the profound peace of God, we must resort to "prayer and supplication." Mastering this prayer of surrender, "Thy Kingdom come. Thy will be done," has two significant implications in our lives:

1. **Understanding and embracing God's plan:** this is at the heart of our spiritual journey. We often find ourselves torn between two paths: our own desires versus God's intentions for us. Most of the time, they don't align. Praying with sincerity, "Thy kingdom come. Thy will be done," is a profound expression of surrender. When we utter these words, we are not praying for others around us. We are asking for God's will to be manifest in our own lives. Accepting God's will isn't straightforward: it's easy to claim acceptance verbally, but truly embracing situations we can't change is a different story. We desire control, especially over situations we find unsettling, whether it's a challenging relationship or a situation at work. But the truth is, a significant portion of our lives unfolds beyond our control. From our birth to aspects of our upbringing, many elements are preordained. And it's not about what we can control, but how we manage what we can't. Constant worrying won't bring peace; no amount of anxiety about a loved one's illness will cure them. The only solution that brings peace in such uncontrollable circumstances is acceptance.

2. **Acceptance:** the only known path to inner peace. If you've discovered another way, I'm eager to hear it! Saint Paul, in Philippians 4:11-13, beautifully captures this sentiment: "For I have learned in whatever state I am, to be content; I know how to be abased, and I know how to abound. Everywhere, and in all things, I have learned both to be full and to be hungry, both to abound and to suffer need. I can do all things through Christ who strengthens me." Contentment is a learned skill, not an innate trait. Reflect on when Saint Paul made this profound statement: not during a vacation, but while imprisoned, constantly accompanied by a Roman guard. Yet, he found contentment through a deliberate choice.

Some may wonder why God doesn't explain His plan, especially when it seems illogical. In our toughest moments, it may feel as if God is silent. Recall grade school exams. During a test, teachers remain silent, only explaining answers afterward. Similarly, God's silence during our personal tests is an invitation to trust in His larger plan. While we might begin our spiritual journey feeling incredibly connected to God, He occasionally steps back, urging us to mature in our faith. This doesn't mean He abandons us, but He challenges us to rely on our faith during His silent moments. In such times, if you find yourself questioning the intensity of your prayers, remember: persistence is key. It's easy to pray when you feel a divine connection, but the true test lies in maintaining faith when you don't. God is always watching. And in response to life's challenges, let us say, "God, Your kingdom come, Your will be done." Trusting Him is the essence of surrender.

Do you know the importance of trusting God, especially when explanations are absent? Trusting Him is vital, not because He will provide an explanation, but because seeking that explanation can become the very barrier to your peace. The desire for clarity from God can prevent you from finding tranquility. Understand this: you might never get that explanation. But why?

Firstly, remember that He is God, and you're not. He doesn't owe you any explanations. He doesn't consult you about changes in your life; He enacts them. The relationship is clear: you answer to Him, not the other way around. Secondly, even if He did provide an explanation, we might not comprehend it. God's wisdom far surpasses ours. In Isaiah 55 God mentions, "as the heavens are higher than the earth, so are my ways higher than your ways, my thoughts higher than your thoughts." We might not always grasp His actions, given our limited understanding. Lastly, explanations don't always comfort. Imagine losing a loved one in an accident. Would knowing the cause, like a drunk driver, truly alleviate your pain? Explanations don't heal wounds. God knows this. Instead of explanations, He offers His unwavering presence, promising to stay with us through thick and thin.

Accepting God's Plan

Understanding the prayer of surrender begins by accepting God's plan. Let me share a story I once encountered in an email. Now I never usually open this sort of thing, but for some reason I did:

A man watched a struggling butterfly trying to free itself from its cocoon. After hours, when the butterfly seemed stuck, out of kindness he cut the cocoon open. The butterfly emerged, but its body was shrunken and wings weak. Unlike other butterflies, it couldn't fly and spent its life crawling. What the man didn't understand was the cocoon's resistance was nature's way of strengthening the butterfly's wings. Without challenges, the butterfly remained weak. Similarly, struggles in our lives are necessary. Without them, we might remain weak. Struggles can be blessings in disguise, fortifying us for future challenges.

Surrender to God's Control

Beyond accepting God's plan, we must also surrender to His control in all facets of our lives. This means letting go before He intervenes. Surrender is a choice: either gracefully accept His will or resist it. Seeking peace requires this surrender. It's common to claim total surrender while holding back a little, thinking, "I've given God control, but I'll handle this detail." This isn't true surrender. Often, this half-hearted commitment is disguised by the phrase, "God wants me to be happy, right?" This can lead to justifying actions that stray from God's path.

Embracing surrender can lead to peace. Romans 8:6 states, "For to be carnally minded is death, but to be spiritually minded is life and peace." And Job 22:21 adds, "Now acquaint yourself with Him, and be at peace; Thereby good will come to you." Peace and goodness stem from truly knowing and surrendering to God's will.

Resentment

Have you ever wondered what prevents most people from fully surrendering to God? It's resentment towards Him, but often, this resentment is unrecognized. It arises from not receiving what we desire or expect. For instance, some may wish they looked different, believing it would make their life better. Others may wish they had different parents, secretly feeling that if God truly cared, He would have given them a different family. It's natural to occasionally feel upset or disappointed with God. However, holding onto that resentment for extended periods is harmful.

Think of it like a cold. A brief cold isn't concerning. But a cold lasting six months? That's a cause for alarm. If you find yourself upset with God for weeks or even months, it's crucial to address that resentment. The key is to move past these feelings, stop blaming God, and embrace the belief that His plans are for the best. A simple prayer might help: "Even when I don't understand, I trust. Thy kingdom come, Thy will be done in my life. I accept Your plan and surrender to Your control."

Trust in God's Care

The next step is trust, particularly trusting in God's care. Isaiah 26:3 says, "You will keep him in perfect peace, Whose mind is stayed on You, Because he trusts in You." Realize that life will never be without challenges. If you think otherwise, you're mistaken. I often see life as an aircraft carrier: each plane circling it represents a problem. As soon as you handle one, another emerges. If you believe peace only comes when problems disappear, you'll never find it. This world is imperfect, and we all make mistakes. The goal is to find peace amidst the chaos, trusting in God's care.

The beauty lies in Matthew 6:33: "But seek first the kingdom of God and His righteousness, and all these things shall be added to you." Prioritize God, trust and surrender to Him, and He will provide for you. Reflect on this: Are you at peace or facing turmoil? If peace eludes you, consider what you need to surrender, accept, or trust in God's care. Identify and address that obstacle, and peace will follow.

The Serenity Prayer

Lastly, let's consider the Serenity Prayer. Most are familiar with its shortened form: "God grant me the serenity to accept the things I cannot change, the courage to change things that I can, and the wisdom to know the difference." Yet, the latter part is truly powerful: "Living one day at a time, enjoying one moment at a time, accepting hardships as a pathway to peace. Taking, as Jesus did, the sinful world as it is, not as I wish it were. Trusting that You will make all things right if I surrender to Your will, ensuring I'm content in this life and blissfully happy with You in the next." Here, the words "accepting," "trusting," and "surrendering" are emphasized. Master these, and you'll find your pathway to peace.

CHAPTER 4

PEACE IN PRAYER

I arrived home late, at 11:30 p.m. after a long day. I had yet to see the kids and attempted to wake one of them up, but my wife advised against it. We spent some quality time together, and later, as I began to wind down, I noticed a helicopter outside my window. Moments later, another one appeared. I mused, "Wait a minute, there can't be a fleet of 55 helicopters. It must be the same one circling." As I suspected, it was. Unsure if it was due to a major accident or some crime scene about 300-400 yards away, I grew curious. However, my wife discouraged me from driving down to get a closer look. Turning to the internet for answers, I stumbled upon tragic news. A bomb had detonated in Egypt, resulting in approximately 88 deaths and leaving hundreds injured. Though the helicopter incident had piqued my interest, this other news deeply disturbed me.

Engrossed, I continued browsing, coming across an article discussing homeland security and its escalating costs over the years. The department, established post 9/11, saw its budget soar from 17 billion to 29 billion and then to 38 billion dollars in consecutive years. The primary goal? Ensuring the country's safety. A related survey revealed that most respondents were even willing to pay higher taxes for enhanced security: people seem ready to invest vast amounts to feel safe and at peace. Yet no agency, sum of money, or technological advancement can truly offer inner peace. This is further supported by statistics, highlighting that 1 in 8 Americans between the ages of 18-54 grapple with anxiety disorders. Today, such disorders have eclipsed depression, solidifying the notion that many are in a relentless pursuit of inner peace amidst external chaos and personal challenges.

Inner peace doesn't equate to global peace. Everyone, regardless of their surroundings or beliefs, experiences anxiety and stress. A common misconception is that attending church, upholding Christian values, or merely being righteous provides immunity from life's pressures. However, true peace requires a deeper understanding of one's faith. As Philippians 4:6-7 promises, "Be anxious for nothing, but in everything prayer and supplication, with thanksgiving, let your requests be made known to God; and the peace of God, which surpasses all understanding, will guard your hearts and minds through Christ Jesus."

Our quest is to understand how prayer aligns with peace, for the Bible asserts that the pathway to God's peace is through prayer. Prayer fundamentally means seeking assistance beyond our own capabilities. It recognizes the limitations in our lives and turns to a higher power for guidance and support. Typically, our prayers lean towards personal requests: "God, give me this. I need that." However, the sequence of the Lord's prayer places God and His attributes first before our desires, suggesting the importance of understanding and honoring who God is before stating our needs.

Seeking God

To find true peace, we must view God as the solution to our needs. It's not merely about bread but the essentials we need to thrive. When we attempt to meet our needs without seeking God, anxiety and stress often follow, eclipsing peace. Only by recognizing God as the ultimate provider can we hope to find solace and provision for our daily needs.

Consider Matthew 7:9-11. Envision yourself as a parent: when your child approaches with a need, how would you respond? "Which of you, if your son asks for bread, will give him a stone? Or if he asks for a fish, will give him a snake? If you, then, though you are evil, know how to give good gifts to your children, how much more will your Father in heaven give good gifts to those who ask him!" There is an innate desire within a parent to meet their child's needs. Yet, just as a loving father knows not to indulge every whim of his child, God distinguishes between our wants and needs. We must therefore differentiate between our needs and wants. While God commits to fulfilling our essential needs, not all our wants are granted.

The phrase "those who ask Him" emphasizes our role in communicating with God, laying our needs before Him. Do we always turn to God first? Sadly, not always. Some barriers prevent us from genuinely seeking God. Misunderstandings about God's nature and the purpose of prayer might be factors. Some view God as distant, a deity of cosmic scale but distant from daily life. With such a perspective, it becomes challenging to sincerely pray, "Give us this day, our daily bread" which should reflect our genuine reliance on God. While God assures us He will meet our needs, this promise comes with conditions. God does not merely provide whatever we desire; we have a role to play.

In the phrase "Give us this day our daily bread," the repetition of the words "day" and "daily" emphasize the necessity of seeking Him continuously, not just once in our lifetime. If you desire sustenance every day, it's essential to humbly approach God with this request daily. The term "daily" puzzled translators when taken from its original Greek – it's a unique word, absent from the rest of the Bible. This term's meaning became clearer in the 1940s with the discovery of the Dead Sea Scrolls, ancient writings from biblical times. Here, "daily" was associated with perishable goods – items that would last for only a day. This suggests that when praying for our "daily bread," we're asking for our immediate needs. God's message: focus on the present and what you require now. In our modern era, items that last just a day are rare. Years ago, grocery shopping was a straightforward affair, but today's megastores like Costco have transformed it into an exercise of excess. Do we genuinely need to stockpile 100 rolls of toilet paper? Our ancestors understood the genuine essence of "daily bread" because they felt its impact. But it's not always about food; our daily bread can represent emotional, relational, financial, or even spiritual reliance on God.

One might wonder, why does God want us to ask daily for our sustenance? Isn't He aware of our innermost desires and needs? The answer isn't about God desiring daily affirmation. It's about us as humans having short memories. Daily prayers serve as reminders of our dependence on Him. If God supplied all we needed for our entire lives today, would we still turn to Him tomorrow? Remember the Israelites in the Old Testament, God provided them with manna daily for forty years. If they tried storing it overnight, it spoiled, teaching them to trust God's provision every day. So, what is your manna? What reminds you daily of your dependence on God? Challenge yourself to identify and reflect on that one aspect of your life where you genuinely say, "God, today I trust You with this."

God's Resources

One key lesson we derive from the verse Philippians 4:19 is the importance of depending on God's abundant resources. The verse beautifully states, "My God shall supply all your need according to His riches in glory by Christ Jesus." Emphasis on the phrase, "His riches in glory." This isn't merely a verse but also a powerful promise. It assures us that God stands prepared to fulfill all our necessities. His resources are boundless. If you seek financial support, remember that God's wealth surpasses any earthly measure. For love or security, God offers it in a magnitude greater than any human can. With His vast riches, God never turns away our genuine needs. Recalling the words from the 'Our Father' we're reminded, "you are my Father in heaven, and I trust that you will meet my needs." It's not just about God's care, but His capability. Just caring wouldn't suffice. For instance, when a loved one has cancer, you might deeply care but lack the means to cure them. The distinction here is between merely wanting to help and actually possessing the means. God possesses both the desire and the means to assist.

Some might ponder: if God promises to meet all needs, why do some remain unfulfilled in life? The answer once again returns to the difference between needs and wants. Imagine a toddler desperately wanting a toy, thinking it's a life-or-death need. Yet, is it truly essential? The disparity between our understanding and a toddler's is similar to our understanding compared to God's. He provides necessities, not indulgences. A responsible parent knows when to say 'no'. They ensure the child's needs are met but might withhold certain wants. God has ensured we never lack. An excerpt from the Gregorian liturgy beautifully conveys this: "you have not left me in need of any of the works of your service." King Solomon's prayer in Proverbs 30:8-9 reflects profound wisdom. He prays, "Give me neither poverty nor riches – Feed me with food allotted to me," indicating a wish for just enough to meet his needs. He fears that abundance might lead him away from God, while scarcity might push him into sin. Such contentment is rare, especially in today's materialistic society. It seems there's always more to chase – be it jobs, cars, or any material possession. May we all learn to find contentment in what we have and trust God to provide just what we need. Saint Paul's words to Timothy in 1 Timothy 6:6-8 encapsulate this sentiment. He writes, "Now godliness with contentment is great gain. For we brought nothing into this world, and it is certain we can carry nothing out. And having food and clothing, with these we shall be content."

Chapter 5

FORGIVE US OUR TRESPASSES

Let us delve into the teachings found within the Lord's Prayer, starting with the phrase "Forgive us our debts." While some are more familiar with it as "Forgive us our trespasses," the use of "trespasses" is rooted in old English vernacular. Interestingly, we've retained this older language in our recitations of the 'Our Father.'

Guilt

Guilt, as an emotion, often stands as a significant obstacle to achieving peace. While it stems from past mistakes and regrets, it's crucial to understand that lingering on these feelings can prevent one from experiencing peace. Guilt and peace are mutually exclusive and cannot coexist. Guilt is uniquely human, separating us from animals. While animals may experience pain or happiness, they lack the moral conscience that burdens us with guilt. Such a sentiment can be severely damaging. It can:

1. Overwhelm you emotionally, leaving you unstable.
2. Weaken you spiritually, affecting self-esteem and potentially leading to depression.

But guilt can also serve as a warning signal, just like the 'check engine' light in a car. It suggests there's an internal issue that needs immediate attention. Neglecting it, just as ignoring the car's warning light, can lead to more significant problems at any moment.

Addressing guilt requires fighting the natural human reaction to mask or deflect it. For instance, if one feels guilty about being rude, the immediate reaction might be to blame the other person. It's easier to point fingers than to accept responsibility. We might also shift blame onto external factors, such as society or individuals from our past to rationalise the behaviour. These strategies however are ineffective. Using the analogy of trying to submerge tennis balls in a pool: no matter how hard one tries to push one down, another pops up. It's an exhausting and futile effort.

The hard question is: how does one genuinely rid themselves of guilt? I once heard a radio talk-show where the host asserted that one couldn't. This is not a notion I support. Our Lord promises us peace, not a life burdened by guilt. The essence of the Lord's Prayer, "Forgive us our debts," emphasizes seeking and understanding forgiveness. Grasping the depth of God's forgiveness and accepting it is the remedy for guilt. Hence, each time we pray, we request God's pardon, acknowledging that true freedom from regret and guilt lies in His grace.

Understanding God's Forgiveness

Many might think, "I've repented countless times, prayed for God's forgiveness, and asked for pardon. Why do I still feel guilty?" If you're praying for God's forgiveness but don't find peace, sorry to say the issue lies with you, not with God. It's never God's failure to keep His promises. Often, the disconnect arises because we might not truly grasp the nature of God's forgiveness. There are four unique aspects of it:

1. **God's Immediate Forgiveness:** When God forgives, it's instantaneous. Unlike humans who might take time to ponder their decision, God doesn't make you wait. As Psalm 86:5 states, "For you, Lord, are good,

and ready to forgive, And abundant in mercy to all those who call upon you." It's challenging for us to comprehend this because we often hesitate before forgiving others. But God doesn't need you to beg or plead. He forgives the moment you ask. And it's as simple as 1 John 1:9 says, "If we confess our sins, He is faithful and just to forgive us our sins and to cleanse us from all unrighteousness." So, how long should Christians feel guilty? Roughly ten seconds—just the time it takes to ask for God's forgiveness. Once forgiven, guilt should dissipate. This counters the common belief that guilt acts as a deterrent.

2. **God's Constant Forgiveness:** Closely linked with His immediate forgiveness is God's willingness to forgive repeatedly. It is our human nature to err repeatedly, so this is a comforting thought. If you've fallen into the same sin repeatedly, you might doubt God's patience. However, Nehemiah 9:17 assures us of His abundant kindness: "But You are God, Ready to pardon, Gracious and merciful, Slow to anger, Abundant in kindness." Hebrews 7:25 further affirms this: "Therefore He is also able to save to the uttermost those who come to God through Him, since He always lives to make intercession for them." He constantly intercedes for us, eager to forgive.

Why Some Hesitate to Repent

Reluctance to bother God: Some believe they shouldn't approach God repeatedly for the same mistakes. I learned a lesson about this when I hesitated to call 911 during a bout of heat exhaustion. I happened to have a friend who was a doctor at my house, who ganged up on me with my wife and told me I had to go to the hospital. I felt I was inconveniencing them. But the responder reminded me that it was their job to help, just as it is God's nature to forgive. Sometimes we do this with God – we don't want to confess because we try to fix the situation first, then think we can return to God. But that never, ever works.

Being "too busy": No one is too busy to seek forgiveness. Equating forgiveness with a valuable treasure, imagine neglecting a billion-dollar prize because you're "too busy." I liken guilt to household garbage. If you don't dispose of trash regularly, your house becomes a mess. Similarly, sins should be repented for daily. And periodically, like taking out the large garbage bins, we should seek confession. The key takeaway is not to keep an accumulating record of sins. If you only addressed your wrongdoings once a year, it would be as unpleasant as taking out trash annually. Strive to keep your inner self as clean as your living space.

God's Freely Given Forgiveness

God offers forgiveness free of charge. While it seems too good to be true, the concept is simple: forgiveness from God is truly free. But, does that mean there's no price associated with it? Is it truly fair to continuously receive something without a price? Let's explore Romans 3:23-24: "For all have sinned and fall short of the glory of God, being justified freely by His grace through the redemption that is in Christ Jesus." Undoubtedly, there's a price for sins and forgiveness, but the good news is you aren't the one footing the bill. However, this doesn't imply obtaining forgiveness comes without a significant cost — the ultimate price was the precious blood of Christ. While forgiveness is freely available to you, remember it's not something you can purchase. Whether you're feeling guilty or tempted to make deals with God, no amount of bargaining will work. God's intention is to give you forgiveness openly and desires to forgive even more frequently than we seek it.

So, if it's freely available, what's required from us? Believe in God's forgiveness and truly accept that you're pardoned. Reflecting on Ephesians 2:8-9: "For by grace you have been saved through faith, and that not of yourselves; it is the gift of God, not of works, that anyone should boast," we're reminded of God's willingness to grant forgiveness without expecting anything in return. I once heard a tale about a boy wishing to purchase the Washington Monument with a mere dollar and some cents. The park ranger responded with wisdom: the monument isn't for sale, and even if it was, the boy couldn't afford it. Yet, as an American, he already owned it. Similarly, God's forgiveness isn't for sale, and even if it was, no human could afford it. Fortunately for Christians, they've already been granted this forgiveness. The root cause of many emotional problems is the inability to accept God's unconditional and free forgiveness.

God's Complete Forgiveness

God's forgiveness is all-encompassing and unwavering. Reflecting on Colossians 2:13-14, it's evident that when God forgives, He wipes the slate clean. There's no partial forgiveness with Him; He is willing to forgive entirely. However, not fully living in this grace, many continue to associate misfortunes with past mistakes, thinking God's punishing them.

It's essential to differentiate between consequence and punishment. Sin will have its punishment, reserved for the afterlife. On Earth, sin results in consequences, not divine punishments: a person's choices lead to outcomes, and these aren't indicators of God's forgiveness. For instance, a woman who becomes pregnant after a one-time mistake faces the consequence of her action, not a punishment from God. Similarly, God disciplined the Israelites to correct their behaviour, not to punish them indefinitely. God's aim is to help us rectify our errors and return to a life of blessing.

When Christ declared, "It is finished," on the cross, He referred to the completion of our redemption. In the original Greek, this phrase translates to "paid in full", emphasizing that Jesus settled our debts with His sacrifice. God's forgiveness may be free for us, but its cost was immense for Him. However, knowing our sins are "paid in full" liberates us from past regrets and guilt. If you still harbor guilt from past sins, it's crucial to repent and then let go, believing in the fullness of God's forgiveness.

Chapter 6

AS WE HAVE FORGIVEN

Let us return our attention to Matthew 6:12, "forgive us our debts, as we also have forgiven our debtors" and explore the latter half: as we also have forgiven our debtors. This has many practical applications as anticipated. While many may not struggle with their relationship with God, the challenge often lies in our relationships with one another. Whether it's a close acquaintance or an aggressive driver on the road, conflicts with others significantly influence our sense of peace. It's common to believe that our peace is disrupted by the actions of others – their mistakes, rudeness, or arrogance. And indeed, people make mistakes. Previously, we considered how to cope with our own errors and the ensuing guilt, emphasizing the remedy is found in God's forgiveness. But what if it is someone else's errors? The solution is mirrored: just as we seek forgiveness, we must also extend it to others. This act of letting go, which I term 'The Prayer of Release,' is crucial to maintaining harmony. Intentionally or not, it's inevitable that others will hurt or upset us; what truly matters however is our reaction. The right response paves the path to peace, while the wrong one leads to internal distress.

The Prayer of Release

To achieve peace, the premise is that we must embrace forgiveness. But a common concern arises: how often should we forgive those who wrong us repeatedly? It's as if we yearn to ask Jesus, "Lord, how many times should I forgive my brother when he wrongs me?" This question was posed by Saint Peter, as recorded in Matthew 18. Peter boldly asked Jesus if forgiving up to seven times – a number he deemed generous, surpassing the Jewish law's requirement of thrice – was sufficient. Jesus recommended not just seven times, but "seventy times seven." This response transcending mere numbers and maths, but rather conveys an essential lesson: true forgiveness of others must be unlimited – just as God gives it to us.

The parable of the unforgiving servant in Matthew 18 highlights the significance of forgiveness and why we should embrace it. The kingdom of heaven is likened to a king who decided to settle his accounts with his servants. As he commenced, one servant who owed him ten thousand talents was brought forward. For comparison, ten thousand talents is akin to 12 million dollars in modern terms! This staggering amount adds to the picture of this servant's seemingly insurmountable debt. To further put this into perspective, even if you paid $1,000 daily for 30 years, you wouldn't clear it. So when the servant couldn't pay, the king ordered him, his family, and possessions to be sold to recoup the debt. This wasn't cruelty, but the prevailing law of the time. In desperation, "the servant therefore fell down before him, saying, 'Master, have patience with me, and I will pay you all.'" Such a promise, given the vast sum, was almost ludicrous. If you or I were to have some compassion, perhaps we would say "OK, I will have mercy on him. I'll make him pay back only half." Or maybe ask for 25%? Remarkably, in a gesture of profound compassion and total plot twist, the king forgave the entire debt. This wasn't about making a bad financial compromise; it was about the king valuing his inner peace rather than pursuing monetary wealth. The real secret here is that without letting go of bitterness, we'll never find true peace. Regardless of our past hurts, we must learn to forgive, not necessarily for the offender's sake but for our own well-being. Forget the notion of "they don't deserve it." The real question is, don't you deserve peace?

Our Obligation to Forgive

God has forgiven each of us, and understanding this will bring peace to our past, present, and future. Reflecting on our past, we realize that God's grace has covered our numerous shortcomings, similar to the incomprehensible compassion shown by the king to cancel the enormous debt of his servant. Though $12 million is a huge sum, it pales in comparison to the depth of forgiveness God offers us. We've all acted thoughtlessly towards Him at some point, yet instead of the punishment we might expect, we've been granted mercy. Is there a catch? God doesn't write blank checks... so yes there is definitely a catch to it. God essentially says: I am willing to write off every single debt that you owe, but you must be willing to do the same with others. Romans 8:1 reveals, "There is therefore now no condemnation to those who are in Christ Jesus, who do not walk according to the flesh, but according to the spirit." This profound forgiveness is something many fail to grasp fully. On the day of judgement, God won't question each of our missteps; He'll simply ask if we repented. We can't plead for God's mercy while withholding it from others who wrong us.

As we continue the parable in Matthew 18, we discover this servant who, after being forgiven an astronomical debt, refused to forgive a relatively minuscule one owed to him. When the debtor begged for patience, echoing the very same plea the servant had made earlier, the servant responded with anger and violence. Why this lack of mercy, especially after receiving such immense compassion? The crux of the matter: he didn't genuinely believe he was forgiven and deep down, likely suspected the master's mercy was temporary. Similarly, our ability to forgive is intrinsically linked to our acknowledgment of God's forgiveness; we nurture bitterness, resentment, or grudges because we haven't truly experienced (or understood) God's grace. Some mistakenly believe that mere acts, like attending church, can earn God's forgiveness. This misunderstanding is not just erroneous but also arrogant: the idea that our actions could repay an infinite debt misunderstands the very nature of grace. Once again to truly forgive others, we must first accept our own forgiveness. It may be a generalisation, but often those who are judgmental or critical are battling unresolved guilt within themselves. To move forward in life, we need to grasp the depth of God's forgiveness and extend it to others. Ephesians 4:32 summarises this perfectly: "Be kind to one another, tender-hearted, forgiving one another, even as God in Christ forgave you."

Resentment

Resentment typically inflicts more pain on the person holding it than the intended target. When you harbor resentment, you become its victim, suffering its side-effects. Many have approached me, saying, "Abouna, I despise this person for their past actions." I explain that holding onto this bitterness lets the person, who might have long moved on, wield power over them. Imagine being controlled by someone who might not even remember you! Why inflict this upon yourself? Feeling that "this person infuriates me," showcases a position of enslavement. You might be surrounded by blessings and comforts, yet somehow another person controls your emotions. By refusing to forgive, you give implicit permission for this to happen. That's unwise. Remember, no one can impact your happiness unless you let them. Instead, empower yourself by choosing forgiveness, recognizing that it lies within your grasp. Forgiveness isn't a fleeting emotion; it's a deliberate choice not just for their benefit but for your own well-being. In the parable of the unforgiving servant, we hear about this self-infliction: "So when his fellow servants saw what had occurred, they were distressed and informed their master. He summoned the servant, rebuking, 'You wicked servant! I forgave your debt because you pleaded. Shouldn't you have shown compassion to your fellow servant, as I did for you?' Angered, the master handed him to the torturers until he repaid his debt." I interpret "delivered him to the torturers" to mean that harbouring resentment is akin to self-torture. Bitterness can sometimes be more debilitating than physical ailments. The destructive nature of resentment resembles that of cancer, growing within you causing damage until there's nothing left. Not only is it spiritually harmful, but the physical toll of resentment is significant: research shows that grudge-bearers have higher risks of strokes, heart attacks, and elevated cholesterol levels. In Job 21, we read how the Scriptures were ahead of scientific findings, illustrating two life trajectories: one marked by contentment and the other tainted by bitterness: "One dies in his full strength, being wholly at ease and secure… Another man dies in the bitterness of his soul, Never having eaten with pleasure."

The Blame and Bitterness Test

This is our next challenge. Ask yourself: With whom are you keeping score? Regardless of their good or bad actions, they can never pay back this imaginary debt in your mind – you will continue to keep count, even for something they did back in 1985 when you were in third grade!

If you find yourself faulting the Blame or Bitterness Test – if you feel a person's mistake keeps you from a harmonious relationship – realize this: the problem is not with them, but it is actually your unwillingness to forgive. Everyone makes mistakes and we all stumble, but these mistakes don't ruin relationships; it's our inability to forgive that does. Just like the parable where a servant's refusal to forgive led him to torment and imprisonment, if you withhold forgiveness, you are shackled by your own bitterness. This self-inflicted cage lets tormentors gnaw at you slowly, and sadly makes us like an old, grumpy and bitter character.

Acknowledging the following is key: you and I will need to be forgiven again, and we must learn to do it because sooner or later I'll seek it from others and from God. "So My heavenly Father also will do to you if each of you, from his heart, does not forgive his brother his trespasses." (Matthew 18:35). Next time you pray, "Forgive us our trespasses, as we forgive those who trespass against us," take a moment to consider its weight. If you plead for forgiveness for your actions but hold onto others' mistakes, be wary of what you're asking for. A man once approached a priest, unable to forgive someone. The priest in his wisdom replied, "Then, my son, may you never sin again." Withholding forgiveness destroys the very path we all need for salvation.

Have You Truly Forgiven Someone?

How do you truly know if you've forgiven someone? While it's often tied to individual situations, there's a general guideline: you have not forgiven them if you can't genuinely stand before God and pray for their well-being. It's not about wishing misfortune upon them, but sincerely hoping for their betterment. If you find it hard to pray for that difficult colleague or the neighbor who gets on your nerves, then perhaps forgiveness is still a work in progress. Of course, your specific situation may require additional things to show forgiveness, but this is the bare minimum.

Look at Matthew 5:7: "Blessed are the merciful, For they shall obtain mercy." God's message is clear: He desires not just isolated acts of forgiveness from us, but a forgiving and merciful spirit. Being forgiving should be a consistent approach to life, not a one-time act. At the heart of Christianity – and what sets it apart from other belief systems – is the essentiality of forgiveness. Forgive and move past the debt. Being forgiven and forgiving are two sides of the Christian coin. It's essential to receive forgiveness from God before you can genuinely offer it to others. If you're not grounded in this dual aspect of forgiveness, your faith is in trouble. The essence of Christianity revolves around God's forgiveness toward us, prompting our forgiveness toward others. Before passing judgment on others, remember your own imperfections. No one has tested God's patience more than I have, yet He continually overlooks my flaws.

Life will undoubtedly bring pain and betrayals. Yet, when hurt, you're faced with a choice: to heal and rise above or to harbor bitterness. We often lament our woes, but the real question is, do we truly want healing or just a platform for our bitterness? Choosing healing often requires collaboration and openness to let go of the hurt, even if it means revisiting painful memories. Constantly reminding yourself of past injuries only perpetuates your suffering. Understand that while they might not seem deserving of your forgiveness, you merit the peace that comes with being forgiving. It's a common misconception that forgiving someone lets them off the hook. But holding onto past hurt isn't penalising them—it's imprisoning you. Trust in God's all-seeing nature. Every wrong done, every injustice felt, He is aware of it. Let go and let Him handle it. You have been forgiven by God in the past, you enjoy His current grace, and will inevitably need His forgiveness in the future. Release the hurt, embrace forgiveness, and find the peace you so rightly deserve.

CHAPTER 7

LEAD US NOT INTO TEMPTATION

Lead us not into temptation, but deliver us from the evil one." Every one of us regularly faces temptation. In fact, if you're human and alive, you've faced temptation within the past 24 hours. We call God the King of Peace, yet this King cannot reside amidst conflict and unrest. When we sin, when we yield to temptation, we push out the King of Peace. We must learn from the prayer, "lead us not into temptation, but deliver us from the evil one," and maintain our inner peace by resisting evil. Few things rob our peace as quickly as succumbing to temptation. It's a somber topic, but one of great significance.

Who is the evil one?

Although it may sound simple, to truly grasp the gravity of this question, we need to look at the bigger picture. More significant than any cosmic battle portrayed in movies like Star Wars or Independence Day, there's a real fight between two beings: God and the devil. The latter is whom God dubs "the evil one." Just as God is real, so is the devil. Often when people think of the devil, they revert back to the childhood cartoon version: a cute, cuddly red guy wearing horns, kind of naughty but fun-loving. That is very, for a lack of a better term, stupid! The real devil – as described in the Bible – is akin to a roaring lion, fierce and ready to destroy. He is out to ruin you, and if you underestimate him, you're in danger. They say the greatest trick the devil ever played was convincing people he doesn't exist. But be vigilant, for he is ever-present, always waiting for an opportunity to lead you astray.

Our Lord described the devil in various ways, emphasizing his cunningness and malevolence. So, in this cosmic battle, what's at stake? Not land, money, or material gains, but our more importantly our souls. Each one of us must realize this war revolves around our soul. The devil desires us for his dark purposes, while God wants us for His divine family. This information isn't meant to frighten but to enlighten. Recognizing the devil and his tactics equips us to resist him better. Hence, every day, we should stand firm in our prayers, acknowledging the presence of evil, and seeking God's protection and deliverance.

Being aware of the devil's tactics increases our chances of resisting him. But what are these tactics? Many may wonder if the devil's weapon is sin. However, the devil cannot impose sin upon us directly so instead, he employs temptations. It's crucial to understand that while the devil can tempt, he can't make us sin. Pointing fingers and claiming, "the devil made me do it" is just an excuse for our actions. It's our choice whether to succumb to temptations or resist them. Our Lord teaches us to pray not to fall into temptation.

Temptation

One might wonder why God allows the devil to tempt us. If He truly wanted us to succeed, why doesn't He prevent these temptations? The intriguing idea is that temptations can be beneficial. It might sound counterintuitive but consider Romans 8:28: "And we know that all things work together for good to those who love God." If everything, including temptation, can work for our good, it suggests that facing temptation can strengthen our faith. But how?

Temptation is often misunderstood. Dictionary.com describes temptation as something seductive or alluring. Picture a shady figure in a movie, lurking in an alley and drawing you into a trap. That's what temptation does – it presents something appealing, misleading you into making wrong decisions. However, being righteous doesn't make you immune to temptation. Even Jesus faced temptation, as seen in Matthew 4:1: "Then Jesus was led up by the Spirit into the wilderness to be tempted by the devil." What's essential is recognizing that temptation isn't a sin; it's yielding to it that is. Temptations are opportunities: respond correctly, and they can draw you closer to God.

An adage likens temptation to birds flying overhead: you can't stop them from flying, but you can prevent them from nesting. It's the same with temptation. It's always present, but our responsibility is to fend it off, preventing it from taking root. Our Lord teaches us to pray daily against temptation. Every significant failure or sin in life began as a minor temptation. Being tempted is not always a sign of weakness or spiritual decline. In fact, it's an indicator that there's a vibrant spirit within you. The presence of temptation suggests an ongoing spiritual battle. If the devil felt he had already claimed you, he wouldn't bother tempting you further. Think of it like a hunter who never seeks prey he already possesses. If you're facing temptation, it means you're still valuable prey, not yet ensnared. Consider a seed. For it to sprout, it must break through the surface, battling against the dirt that surrounds it. The effort required to push through is evidence of life within. In a similar way, your battle against temptation shows there's spiritual life in you. If someone claims they're spiritually sound but face no temptations, it might imply spiritual stagnation.

How to handle temptation

There are two methods to deal with temptation: man's way and God's way. Usually the cycle goes as follows: we try man's way because it's the natural way, and then when it fails we become desperate and try God's way.

Option A is man's way, the conventional human response to temptation is simple: "just don't do it". This mentality is shallow and usually ineffective. It's equivalent to deciding to lose weight by suddenly avoiding desserts. The fact is, resisting temptation is not about sheer willpower. Temptations tend to strike at our weakest moments, not when we're strong. The devil doesn't fight fair; he targets us when we're vulnerable, especially during personal or financial crises. Temptations intensify during such times, rendering the "just stop" mentality useless.

This isn't to downplay the role of willpower. But, while it's essential, it's not enough on its own. If it were, our faith would be a self-help cult rather than a religion. Christianity centers on our recognition that we need divine intervention. We're like hospital patients; while a positive attitude aids recovery, it can't replace surgery. A hopeful heart can't unblock clogged arteries, just as willpower alone can't save us from sin.

Option B is God's way; understanding human limitations, God's method can be characterized by the following four principles:

1. **Reconnect with God:** start by recognizing God as the source of life and purpose of our existence. The goal of life isn't merely to avoid wrongdoings. Imagine on my deathbed (at 115 years old) someone asks, "Fr. Anthony, did you live a meaningful life?", and I merely answer that I refrained from wrong deeds, it speaks of a shallow and meaningless life. The goal is not just to never do bad things, the goal is to be filled with God, and live for God's purposes and find that relationship with God. If you're going to college, the goal is to get A's, B's, it's not just to go in and not fail. Similarly, our spiritual journey isn't about merely avoiding sins, but building a connection with God. Consider Colossians 1:16, which states, "For by Him all things were created that are in heaven and

on earth... All things were created through Him and for Him". Life presents a grand narrative where God and the devil contend for our souls. The devil's goal isn't merely to lead us to addiction or infidelity; it is to disconnect us from God, leading to our spiritual downfall. Recognizing this, the first step in handling temptation is to fortify our connection with God, being vigilant that temptation seeks to weaken this bond. If we face temptations without God's strength, we will certainly be defeated.

2. **Flee from Temptation:** while it may sound straightforward, avoiding temptation is challenging. Facing temptation head-on isn't the solution. The devil, who is described as a roaring lion, will overpower anyone daring to confront him. Scripture doesn't instruct us to resist or combat temptation, so what does it tell us to do? 2 Timothy 2:22 advises, "Flee all youthful lusts". In moments of temptation, it's wise to retreat swiftly, exactly as one would run away from a lion rather than stay and fight it. Anytime the Bible speaks about a certain character like Moses or Elijah, all of them have weaknesses which the Bible doesn't hide. But there's only one character I can think of that I find didn't make any mistakes, and that's Joseph. In the Old Testament he was in my opinion the most Christ-like character in the Bible. One thing Joseph mastered more than anyone else was fleeing from temptation. One day, Potiphar's wife came to him and tried to seduce him, so what does he do? "But it happened about this time, that Joseph when he went into the house to do his work, and none of the men of the house was inside, that she caught him by his garment, saying, "Lie with me." But he left his garment in her hand, and fled and ran outside." (Genesis 39:11-12). He didn't rationalize or debate; he simply ran, understanding the gravity of the temptation. Temptations are like fires, captivating

but perilous. Succumbing to them burns not just the skin, but jeopardizes the soul. Thus, when faced with temptation, it's best to distance oneself immediately. In the financial world, debt relief companies advise struggling clients to cut up credit cards to avoid further debt.

Addressing our inner struggles After avoiding immediate temptation, our next step is to address our internal issues. Temptations often reveal deeper challenges we face. For example, the high school girl who sleeps around and has sex with different guys, her problem may be a bad relationship with her dad, or she never felt love growing up, or something even more complex. The problem is not the sexual behaviour, the problem is on the inside. Similarly, an alcoholic's addiction might stem from low self-esteem or other struggles. Most temptations or sins are external manifestations of internal problems and therefore we need to address these internal issues rather than just the outward symptoms. A father of confession can help in this area, as it is very difficult to do independently, but with the help of others, we can try to go deeper. This is where temptation can actually be a good thing; temptation here can be used as an opportunity for growth, peace, and even for good. If I'm smart and I see that this temptation causes this problem, and I'm able to solve this problem, I'm a better person because of it. Ultimately, every temptation presents a choice: to move away from goodness or closer to it. At its core, it's a choice between aligning ourselves with God or straying away. "Woe to you, scribes and Pharisees, hypocrites! For you cleanse the outside of the cup and dish, but inside they are full of extortion and self-indulgence. Blind Pharisee, first cleanse the inside of the cup and dish, that the outside of them may be clean also" (Matthew 23:25-26). Similarly, we should address our internal challenges to truly overcome our temptations.

3. **The Importance of Seeking Support:** one of the devil's greatest deceptions is making us believe we can combat temptations alone. We need support to overcome them. As James 5:16 advises, "Confess your trespasses to one another, and pray for one another, that you may be healed. The effective, fervent prayer of a righteous man avails much". We benefit from the support of others, and not just from confessors. Spiritual fathers, close friendships, and supportive church communities are crucial. Facing challenges alone makes us vulnerable, but with these connections we are stronger. Ecclesiastes 4:12 tells us, "Though one may be overpowered by another, two can withstand him. And a threefold cord is not quickly broken". This wisdom reminds us that together, we can face and overcome challenges. Temptations are inevitable, but with the right approach and support, we can navigate them faithfully. Always remember, in times of temptation, you're never truly alone. God accompanies and watches over you closer than you might think. "Then Jesus was led up by the Spirit into the wilderness to be tempted by the devil" (Matthew 4:1). Jesus too faced temptation, guided by the Holy Spirit. God's presence is a reassurance that you're not alone in your battles. Furthermore, 1 Corinthians 10:13 assures us, "No temptation has overtaken you except such as is common to man; but God is faithful, who will not allow you to be tempted beyond what you are able, but with the temptation will also make the way of escape, that you may be able to bear it".

Trust in God's guidance and protection, take him along on your journey. His desire is not to see us falter but to guide us safely through our trials.

Chapter 8

FOR THINE IS THE KINGDOM, AND THE POWER, AND THE GLORY

When we pray, many of us do not achieve peace; not because of a lack of sincerity, but because we might not be praying correctly. Using Jesus' model prayer, let us analyze the final phrase: "For Thine is the kingdom, and the power, and the glory, forever. Amen." I refer to this as "The Prayer of Blessing."

Take, for example, the popular movie series "Indiana Jones." The protagonist, Indiana Jones, is on a quest for "the Holy Grail," believed to be the cup used by Jesus during the Last Supper. Throughout the movie, his goal continually seems just beyond his grasp. Just when it appears within reach, obstacles arise, making it seem ever-elusive. Similarly, the idea of "Blessing" can be likened to Jones's search. Everyone is in pursuit of blessings, but just as they feel close, it often slips away. Some might spend their entire lives chasing the idea of a "true" blessing without ever understanding its essence. Regardless of religious belief, people universally desire God's blessing because it's transformative. If I am impoverished and lacking but possess God's blessing, I am content. Conversely, one might have fame and fortune, but without God's blessing, life feels empty.

You may wonder why some seem enveloped in God's grace while others face hardships? Some people's endeavors always seem blessed: whether in academics, family life, or other ventures. What's the reason for this disparity? Is it luck? Favoritism from God? Or perhaps a cursed life? The answer is none of the above. The Lord's Prayer's concluding phrase offers insights into accessing these blessings. It outlines three tenets for a blessed life: seeking God's kingdom, relying on His power, and living for His glory.

Seeking God's Kingdom

This requires dedication to God's purpose, deciding in life that "my whole life goal is to do whatever God wants me do". Instead of asking, "Lord, bless my plans," we should pray, "Lord, guide me towards what You want to bless." It's a shift from seeking God's approval for our choices to seeking His direction. Pursuing God's kingdom is about aligning with His concerns and priorities. Jesus imparted this wisdom during the Sermon on the Mount (Matthew 5-7). He spoke of worldly anxieties and encouraged us to prioritize God above all else. He promised that when we put God first, our needs will be met. As Matthew 6:33 states, "Seek first the kingdom of God and His righteousness, and all these things shall be added to you."

Whatever aspect of your life you desire God's blessing in, prioritize Him in that very area. Whether it's your struggling career, strained marriage, or any other realm of your life, place God at the forefront. In every dimension – emotionally, mentally, physically, spiritually, or socially – He seeks that primary position. A nice acronym is the word "first" which explains five areas we need to put God first (but we usually don't):

- **Finances:** Clearly, if you aspire for God to bless your financial life, it's crucial to give generously, primarily through tithes and even beyond. Bottom line is that we say that we love God, and God says that if you love Me, literally put your money where your mouth is. It's not about God needing our money; it's about Him wanting our committed hearts. Genuine blessings come to those who prioritize God over their financial constraints.

- **Interests:** Whether it's your career, hobbies, or leisure activities, ensure God occupies the primary spot. Anything becomes problematic when it overshadows God. TV itself is not bad, however, too much TV may cause you to prioritize it over God, and that's when TV is bad.

- **Relationships:** Prioritize God in all your relations – be it friendships, family, business partnerships, or romantic commitments. In fact, I often joke with my wife, desiring to be her "number two". That's because God alone should fulfill the "number one" role in our lives. No human can entirely meet another's needs; it's God who nourishes us, with loved ones adding to that fulfillment.

- **Schedule:** Your daily routines and plans should reflect God's significance in your life. Just as you 'tithe' money, consider 'tithing' your time. Start each day by connecting with Him and dedicate the beginning of each week, like attending Sunday church. There's never an excuse to miss church on Sunday, because God in the Old Testament commanded the day of the Sabbath. If you're saying that there is a reason you can miss the Sabbath, then you're also saying there's a reason that you can murder, commit adultery, lie and so on. Missing church is akin to disregarding God's other commandments. The essence is to resonate your devotion in actions that don't just favor us, but God.

- **Troubles:** In times of adversity, instead of panicking thinking "how am I going to fix this", turn to God. Rather than being the last resort, prayer should be the first option. In every challenge, ensure God remains your guiding light.

If God genuinely occupies the first place in these five areas of your life, you're on the right path. However, if He's sidelined in even one aspect, it's a wake-up call to reassess your priorities.

Relying on His Power

God's blessings are intertwined with His power: those who lean on this power are the ones He blesses. Psalm 84:5 tells us, "Blessed is the man whose strength is in You." Sometimes God tends to squeeze us into a corner, and nine times out of ten, it is to remind us to rely on His power; if we're not squeezed, we will never rely or depend on Him. Blessings are reserved for those who place their trust and strength in God.

Galatians 3:9 says, "So then those who are of faith are blessed with believing Abraham". Abraham's faith in the Old Testament serves as a powerful example. Just as Abraham was blessed for his unwavering faith and obedience, so too will those who follow in his footsteps. Ask yourself: in what aspects of life are you currently relying on God? Remember, relying on God and yourself simultaneously isn't feasible; it's either one or the other. Matthew 9:29 states, "According to your faith, let it be to you". Without faith, one can't expect blessings. By learning to trust God and lean on His strength, blessings will come.

Relying on God might not come naturally to everyone. For many, the instinct is to solve problems independently. Yet, there are ways to cultivate this reliance on God. Just as muscles are strengthened by resistance training in the gym, spiritual growth comes from facing challenges. That's why God allows us to face seemingly insurmountable obstacles – to refine and strengthen our faith.

The Bible is filled with stories of those who took leaps of faith. Take Moses, for instance. As he led the Israelites out of Egypt, they found themselves trapped between the Red Sea and Pharaoh's forces. In this desperate moment, Moses told the people to "stand still, and see the salvation of the Lord" (Exodus 14:13). However, God had other plans. He instructed Moses to move forward, emphasizing the importance of action. True faith requires stepping out, even when the path isn't clear. As the Israelites advanced, the Red Sea parted, but this miraculous event wouldn't have occurred if they had simply waited passively. Genuine faith means taking proactive steps, even amidst uncertainty. Jeremiah 17:7 says, "blessed is the man who trusts in the Lord, and whose hope is the Lord." Like Moses, we too can experience God's blessings when we move forward in faith. Consider what steps of faith you need to take: perhaps it's a commitment to regular worship or resisting certain temptations. Regardless, trust that God will guide and sustain you.

Living for His Glory

God delights in those who live for His glory. The essential question is: who do you want to shine – yourself or God? If you seek God's blessings, live for His glory. Recall the parable of the talents in Matthew 25. Those who used their talents for God's glory were commended. Similarly, we each have unique gifts given to us by God. Use them to serve and uplift others, which in turn glorifies God. If you're not using your gifts to serve, you're missing out on opportunities to bless others and be blessed in return. It's simple: the more you use your talents to serve, the more you'll be blessed. Blessings aren't found in selfish pursuits but in selfless service. Whether it's welcoming someone at church or assisting in a community project, every act of kindness brings glory to God.

God's blessings aren't based on our skills, wealth, or abilities. He blesses a willing spirit. Embrace His will, depend on His power, and live for His glory. By doing so, there's no limit to what God can do in your life. As John 13:17 says, "If you know these things, blessed are you if you do them". Blessings are within reach so the question is: are you willing to pursue them?

May we remind ourselves that we neglect prayer because we look at it in the wrong way. We must instead work hard to reframe the way we look at it: prayer is an unmissable invitation to build a house, where Jesus assures us of his presence. He promises to come and spend time with us, dine with us, discuss things with us; therefore each room in this house must be constructed to perfection to serve its unique purpose.

Glory be to God. Amen.

Scan the QR code to go to our website where you will find

Book reviews

Great deals

Our full library of books

www.ingramcontent.com/pod-product-compliance
Lightning Source LLC
Chambersburg PA
CBHW030907170426
43193CB00009BA/759